ROUTLEDGE LIBRARY EDITIONS:
JAPAN

MADE IN JAPAN

MADE IN JAPAN

GUENTHER STEIN

Volume 18

Routledge
Taylor & Francis Group
LONDON AND NEW YORK

First published in 1935

This edition first published in 2011
by Routledge
2 Park Square, Milton Park, Abingdon, Oxon, OX14 4RN

Simultaneously published in the USA and Canada
by Routledge
711 Third Avenue, New York, NY 10017, USA

Routledge is an imprint of the Taylor & Francis Group, an informa business

British Library Cataloguing in Publication Data
A catalogue record for this book is available from the British Library

ISBN 13: 978-0-415-56498-4 (Set)
eISBN 13: 978-0-203-84317-8 (Set)
ISBN 13: 978-0-415-58524-8 (Volume 18)
eISBN 13: 978-0-203-84561-5 (Volume 18)

Women working in Pharmaceutical Company

Note the modern apparatus and the old-fashioned hair-dressing, mostly worn at New Year's time

MADE IN JAPAN

BY

GUENTHER STEIN

LONDON: METHUEN & CO. LTD.

36 Essex Street W.C.2

First published in 1935

PRINTED IN GREAT BRITAIN

CONTENTS

ILLUSTRATIONS

EXCHANGE RATES

The rate of exchange of the yen at par (gold parity) is

1 yen = 2*s*.

The 'present rate of exchange' in this book means the average rate during 1934–5: which is

1 yen = 1*s*. 2*d*. to 1*s*. 2½*d*.

CHAPTER ONE

THE DANGER SIGNAL

HOW DID THEY DO IT?

LESS than a century ago the inhabitants of the Japanese islands were forbidden to trade with other countries. To-day a powerful stream of Japanese manufactures is flooding the markets of the world.

The rapid rise of Japan as an industrial nation in the modern sense has been vastly accelerated during the past few years. Established interests of the older exporting countries are menaced by a competitor whose prices are absurdly low, and whose sales methods are amazingly successful.

No longer is the export trade of Japan confined to a short list of articles such as cotton piece goods, toys, paper goods, &c. She is now exporting turbines and motor-cars, wireless sets and bicycles, and she is to-day the second largest producer of artificial silk in the world. She competes with Western exporters by quoting prices which are not merely 10 or 15 per cent lower than theirs, but which may amount to less than one-half, and sometimes to less than one-quarter. Merchants are beginning to say that some Japanese goods are so cheap that they are not worth handling.

How is it possible that Japan, who has to import nearly all her raw materials from abroad, can export manufactured articles at such amazing prices? Are her workers underpaid? Does she use the depreciation of her currency as a premium on exports? Is Japanese industry subsidized by the State? Is the industrial and commercial organization of Japan more efficient than that of her competitors?

To all these questions we shall try to give replies based on a personal, unprejudiced study of Japanese conditions.

There is one more question which preoccupies industrialists of the West even more than the mystery of Japan's low prices. Is the comet-like rise of Japan's export trade a temporary episode, a mere flash in the pan, produced by the desperate spurt of an ambitious nation—or is Japan's economic and political structure strong enough to support the effort for a long time to come? The answer, which is of vital importance to the industrial future of the Western world, can only be conjectured. But from the investigation many lessons arise which may not be without value for the harassed manufacturers and traders of the West.

THE NEW SCARE—AND THE OLD

Japan has made such conquests on world markets because she has developed her own country and her own industries. Her success reflects the industrial coming of age of a junior member of the family of nations. Her progress has been felt so quickly and so keenly owing to the world depression. Even before the depression, Japan had already caused great inconvenience to older industrial countries, and the trouble would have grown even if trade had remained normal. It will probably continue until world prosperity is fully restored.

It is not the first time that Great Britain and other industrial countries have been alarmed by the industrial coming of age of another great nation. About forty years ago a new producer, demanding and finding markets, suddenly appeared in the international community of manufacturers, upsetting a delicate balance of supply and demand, and creating a scare which had much in common with the present fear of Japan.

That new producer was Germany, whose industrial machine had gradually been completed. The skill of German workers challenged that of the British; cheap German products began to force their way into all corners of the globe, pushing aside the manufactures of other countries. And Germany's competitors hoped to warn off potential buyers of German goods with the stamp 'made in Germany'.

The situation was somewhat analogous. In Germany, at that time, the domestic market was as restricted as the Japanese market is to-day, for production increased too rapidly to be absorbed by so poor a country, and much that was produced had to be exported. People in England complained about incredibly low German prices; about low German wages; about German dumping and State subsidies to export; about the imitation of foreign products and trade marks; about the new competitor's dangerously effective pioneering enthusiasm. These grievances were discussed again and again in the House of Commons and in the Press; and the fathers of many of the present British unemployed may have lost their jobs because of German competition.

Great Britain, being the first Power to become industrialized, was able to find employment for her growing population and for her increasing capital by creating new industries and building up foreign markets in a world where large areas remained a 'No Man's Land'. Germany and Japan, with similar domestic problems, were faced with entirely different world conditions.

It was not by chance that no 'American scare' was created in Europe by the industrialization of the United States, organized on a much larger scale than that of either Germany or Japan. For the increased production in this large and wealthy country was intended mainly for domestic consumers, and did not immediately affect world markets. The high wages paid in America continued to keep the country for long outside foreign trade competition.

The sudden success of Germany and Japan

on world markets occurred simultaneously with the political awakening of these countries. Both tried to gain influence and power beyond their frontiers, and both loudly proclaimed their dissatisfaction with the international *status quo*.

On the other hand, America's sudden awakening was accompanied by the conquest of markets within her own boundaries or by an entry into relatively unopened markets beyond her frontiers. America's rise to power did not disturb the world's political or economic balance.

The German scare gradually died down after the close of the century. Or did it merely recede to the background during the happy period of a general boom, though it was even then suspected that this boom could not last for ever?

Or did the differences between goods 'made in Germany' and those 'made in England' and elsewhere help to develop the international atmosphere in which political ambitions, misunderstandings, apparent accidents and diplomatic mistakes could finally result in the World War?

Was this World War perhaps fundamentally a struggle centred round international trade, which it destroyed for so long; a struggle, though perhaps an unintentional one, between junior and senior participants in world trade?

These questions arise when it is said that just as the German scare gradually abated towards the end of the century, the Japanese scare, too, will be 'self-liquidating'. 'Such scares die a natural death.' But perhaps they do not, unless their causes are removed by a strong, more or less planned expansion of world trade and world prosperity which enables newcomers and established industrial countries to develop side by side —unless all are given more room, far more room than they had before the World War, than they have to-day. . . .

JAPAN'S SECRETS

It was not difficult to understand why Germany succeeded in the 'eighties and 'nineties. She was a country geographically near to England, and her inhabitants were a kindred people, though not as advanced politically or economically as the English.

Japan, on the other hand, seems new and strange, and difficult to understand. The country is so far away, so little known. The Japanese are the first among the non-European races of the world to have achieved an independent industrial success. Japan is the first country in which modern industrialization seems to emerge directly from feudalism. Socially and economically she is as puzzling to Western observers as she sometimes appears in the political field.

Japan has succeeded in rapidly learning to produce a great variety of goods. To-day that variety is even larger than her exports would indicate.

Japan has succeeded in developing her large modern industries side by side with home and small-sized industries in a way which has never before been achieved. She has linked up these two types of industries so that they function, if not without friction, at any rate at a profit. And the productive equipment of both types of industry is fast improving.

Japan has succeeded in creating the cheapest labour supply in the world from her large and adaptable population; at the same time her traditional, inexpensively run civilization has enabled her workers to maintain a standard of life which, as a whole, is higher than that maintained in many other industrial countries. Japan's labour reserves, which appear to be inexhaustible, will supply cheap labour for any amount of industrial expansion in the future.

Japan has succeeded in turning her financial difficulties into an asset: her 'controlled inflation' has at least temporarily stimulated her export trade.

The Japanese Government has succeeded in stimulating industry and the export trade in many ways, and watches more jealously than any other Government over its well-being.

The large Japanese concerns have become partners and supporters of the State in the great patriotic drive for industrial expansion and for the development of export trade. They have been able to redress certain disadvantages of the small units existing in the lower spheres of

Japanese industry by co-ordinating them on a higher level.

Finally, Japan has succeeded in turning her shortage of raw materials into a driving force behind her export trade; and she is now trying to safeguard her exports by making political use of her increasing raw-material purchases abroad. Japan has rediscovered the world; she sends export pioneers to the remotest countries, and she tries to win more and more customers for her increasing variety of export goods.

These developments may appear to be the outcome of a great, ingenious plan; actually Japan is perhaps farther removed from a real system of 'planned enonomy' than she is from a system of completely uncontrolled '*laissez-faire*'. What seems to be complete harmony is merely the result of many difficulties and paradoxes, which cancel each other out only to create each other anew.

Japan's progress appears to be the premeditated attack of a stable, though not wealthy people on the trade of other countries. Yet it arises only from the instinctive efforts of a poor and small country, overshadowed by anxieties and difficulties, at least to maintain the present standard of living of her growing population; and if possible to raise it to a level more commensurate with the continuously rising productivity and cultural level of the masses.

Increasing Japanese exports have alarmed the Western World, unable to provide sufficient opportunities for its own traders, much less to make room for a newcomer; but the growing resistance to Japanese exports has created an equally great scare in Japan. The Japanese, from the humblest industrial worker to the managing director of the largest concern, from the liberal politician to the most extreme military enthusiast, are all demanding for Japan expansion on world markets. Japan is convinced that she cannot live without such expansion.

CHAPTER TWO

THE PRODUCTS OF THE TWO JAPANS

STEEL CHAIRS AND HOUSE SHRINES

IN the furniture departments of the numerous large stores of Tokyo, built and managed according to modern American standards, you can buy side by side modern easy chairs made of steel, writing-desks, wardrobes, everything in fact which is used in normal Western households—as well as old Japanese house shrines, cupboard-like miniature temples covered with lacquer, gold and carvings. These shrines, costing from 6 to 600 yen, are used according to ancient rite for offerings of rice, flowers or water in honour of Japan's most important deity Amaterasu-o-mikami, or of the immortal souls of the family's ancestors.

There are also small open coal basins to contain glowing charcoal. They are used to boil the water for tea, and in the winter these coal basins are the only heating device round which the members of the family can warm their hands. One can also buy large flat bamboo baskets, beautifully woven, which take the place of upright wardrobes, and are used for keeping Japanese clothes; and *tatami*, straw mats, to be stretched across framework upholstered with straw, and used to carpet the house. Small chests of drawers and low tables, which complete the furnishings necessary in a Japanese home, are also displayed.

In the bedding departments of these stores the display is equally varied. Elaborate modern mahogany bedsteads as well as inexpensive ones with spring mattresses, pillows and other Western fittings are shown side by side with *futon*, Japanese beds, usually consisting of two quilts put on the mat-covered floor, a huge quilt kimono for winter wear and one or two other quilts, all covered with the same material, and placed on top of the kimono-clad sleeper. Then there are hard pillow rolls for men, and hard little benches for women, who rest their necks on them when they go to sleep so that their high elaborate coiffure will not be disarranged.

In the clothing departments one can buy Western garments for men, women and children, in the latest fashions: cheap suits and expensive suits, costumes, coats, pullovers, shirts, collars and every conceivable article of clothing. One can also purchase pieces of material cut in the proper lengths for women's kimonos. These materials are displayed in thousands of patterns, colours and qualities, suitable for the various seasons and appropriate to the age and purse of the individual buyer. Then there are strips of material for the *obi*, the bright broad belts, worn knotted at the back, which are more important and more expensive than the kimonos themselves; and severe dark materials—silk, wool, and cotton—for men's kimonos for everyday wear and for special ceremonial occasions. *Haori* are displayed, too—they are light Japanese overcoats, made in different colours and models for men and women—and simple dark-blue uniforms, the obligatory garment for schoolboys and students.

In the footwear department one finds shoes for every day, for golf and evening wear in Western styles; socks and stockings made of silk, artificial silk, wool or cotton—all in the latest fashions. And side by side with these one sees *geta*, strong wooden boards, a little broader and shorter than the foot, with two low wooden cross-pieces underneath for good weather, while very high cross-pieces are used on rainy days. There are similar but more modern foot-boards called *zori*, which are made of straw padding, cork, or rubber; and *tabi*, the Japanese socks for men, women and children. The footwear departments also display a huge variety of slippers, which the Japanese put on when they remove their street shoes at the door of their homes.

The departments for household goods are crowded with electric stoves, electric irons, lamps, Western china and hardware, cut glass, coffee machines, tin-openers, and every con-

1. One of the typical small iron workshops
2. Home manufacturing and retail shop of house shrines

ceivable patented article displayed in European shops. Side by side with these goods there is an astonishing variety of neat bamboo articles, curious rice cookers with huge thick wooden lids, and boxes with tea sets for ceremonial use.

The most up-to-date office equipment and writing material can be purchased in the stationery departments, where many varieties of fountain-pens, patent pencils and other articles sold in the West are displayed. Side by side with these one sees piles of writing-brushes which, though inexpensive, are minor works of art. There is also Indian ink; beautiful little receptacles for water; small bowls, in the traditional shape, in which the ink is mixed; lovely, old-fashioned Japanese writing-paper, decorated in many colours and made up into rolls, sheets, pads or books; and curious envelopes used for the traditional social correspondence.

Next to these things there are Western typewriters with Latin script, or with *kana* letters, including about fifty signs, in which the Japanese can transcribe their complicated Chinese script. Then there are very complicated Japanese typewriters, which are surprisingly easy to use and not much more expensive than those with Latin letters. They have a huge keyboard, from which two or three thousand of the Chinese characters in use can be easily selected, so that the most difficult copy can be typed in good Japanese.

In the departments for musical instruments one

can buy gramophones, wireless sets, violins, pianos, mouth-organs and instruments for jazz bands, as well as old-fashioned, romantic Japanese instruments, which are used in the temples and shrines, and at religious festivals and ceremonies. Records from operas, jazz, European classics, military marches and the melancholy beautiful songs of Old Japan are played for the customers.

The provision departments sell commodities only recently adopted for Japanese use, such as coffee, chocolate, sugar, wheat flour, butter, meat, tinned goods and manufactured foodstuffs, everything in fact which forms a part of an ordinary Western diet. In addition, these departments display enormous sacks of rice, tall stacks of all sorts of dried fish and seaweeds, of strangely smelling pickles, radishes, prepared according to the old tradition, lotus and bamboo shoots and many condiments: barrels full of elaborately prepared bean curd and *sake* (rice wine); huge bottles of soy sauce, and neat little wooden boxes with tiny compartments containing assorted Japanese delicacies—salty, spicy or sweet.

MADE IN JAPAN

Most of these commodities, modern and old-fashioned alike, are made in Japan. Almost all of them, as well as the many other goods which complete the stock of a modern Japanese department store, are apparently of fairly good quality, and most of them are much cheaper than they would be anywhere in the West. These goods are provided mainly for Japanese consumers, for even in Tokyo the number of foreigners is insignificant.

A few things used in the West are not yet manufactured in Japan, but the Japanese have at least begun to use everything now produced in the West, though the demand for these goods is still confined to comparatively small numbers in the cities. Every year, however, the list of modern industrial products manufactured in Japan lengthens. This does not mean that the production of specifically Japanese goods is shrinking. On the contrary, every year a greater variety, as well as a greater quantity, of traditional articles are produced by modern methods. In fact, modern industrial ideas and production methods are used to preserve the old traditions. The economic drive behind this development is a recognition of the fact that the standard of efficiency of the masses and their purchasing power must be increased as much as possible, while the cost of living must not be allowed to rise. With this end in view Western shoes of rubber and leather are being manufactured, while simultaneously the use of the cheap *tabi*, worn by the masses, is encouraged by making them with rubber soles, which are more durable. Again, modern fountain-pens are produced, but so are cheap belts to which tin receptacles for a brush and ink are attached, so that Japanese tradesmen can write either in the traditional or the modern manner. There are innumerable similar examples.

In many ways Japan, old-fashioned and modern, traditional and progressive at the same time, is to-day leading a ‘ double ’ life. In this chapter the ‘ double ’ life of her manufacturing industries in regard to the variety and quality of their products will be discussed.

Probably no industrial country produces such a variety of commodities as the Japan of to-day, one of the youngest and poorest amongst them. She makes not only battle-ships, aeroplanes, and motor-cars, but she has also preserved and expanded her own old-style production of typically Japanese goods. As a rule this fact is disregarded, though it is vital to an understanding of Japan’s present and future competitive power on world markets. This industrial dualism has both advantages and disadvantages with regard to Japan’s efforts to increase her export trade.

Modern Japan’s inventive talent, her workmanship and her capital as well as her potential markets have thus to satisfy two distinct demands—(1) for Western goods and (2) for traditional Japanese goods—while her older, more experienced and financially stronger competitors in the West are freed from this complication. It should be emphasized, furthermore, that the production of the innumerable commodities manufactured solely for Japan’s home market is not confined to small plants employing craftsmen, and economically and socially representing the 'old' Japan. On the contrary, the manufacture of these goods has been one of the chief tasks of modern Japanese factories. The variety, and more especially the quality, of the Western goods made in Japan were considerably impaired for a long time by this dual demand. The result was that foreigners underestimated the capacity for development of modern Japanese industry.

The dual character of Japan's industrialization has, however, had certain advantages. By supplying two different demands, modern methods of production and the new technique of the machine age took root more quickly in Japan than would otherwise have been possible. For her industries would have developed more slowly if they had been entirely dependent upon the development of foreign trade or the replacement of traditional goods by Western products, for the latter are usually more expensive. And they are not easy to introduce in Japan where the style of life and work is fundamentally different from that of the West and tradition is very strong.

Many workshops and factories, which were technically revolutionized and reorganized for the production of specifically Japanese commodities, have since become producers of Western export commodities. In Osaka, one large modernized factory produces the bulk of Japan's total requirement of *tabi* hose. It has supplanted the widely spread home industry which formerly produced this typically Japanese footgear. As Japan is rapidly adopting European stockings the factory is not only manufacturing these but is now even exporting them. To-day many products of the 'old' Japan are manufactured in the large factories of the 'new' Japan, while the majority of export goods are produced in the somewhat modernized workshops and factories of the 'old' Japan. It was the development of these small workshops which in recent years has so rapidly increased the variety of goods now made in Japan.

From now on the advantages derived by Japan from the dual character of her industrial production promise increasingly to outweigh the disadvantages. As she completes her dual apprenticeship, the peculiarity of her industry will enable her to expand the variety of her exports and to improve their quality. Presumably, too, she will increase her production at least as quickly as her markets will absorb it.

WORKMANSHIP

By tradition Japan produces goods of excellent quality. More than 300 years ago the Portuguese, the first Europeans to trade with Japan, were buying from her iron nails and plates for shipbuilding, swords, broadswords, spears, porcelain and lacquer ware. Articles made by Japanese craftsmen in the present or in the past, whether cheap or costly, are never crude. A writing-brush, a woven basket, a cup, a wooden bowl, a pair of Japanese scissors, which are made in one piece, a metal tea-pot, Japanese tools and other household utensils, all these articles are beautiful, practical, durable and perfect of their kind. And the use of Japan's best and most expensive products shows them to be in many cases hardly inferior to comparable products of other countries, although they are rarely superior. The average quality of modern Japanese products is fairly good and rapidly improving. The longer an industry has been in existence the better are its products.

Both categories of goods, however, the typical products of Japanese craftsmanship and the best and most expensive products of her modern industry, are exported only in small quantities if at all. The world has judged the quality of Japanese goods by the mass production of her artisans and small-scale manufacturers and by the cheapest goods now being manufactured by modern Japanese industry. Even when the low prices are taken into consideration, the judgment is often unfavourable. It seems that to-day Japanese goods are, on the whole, considered to be of poor quality, and that, for this reason, Japan's future competitive ability is not taken too seriously.

Once before the world made a mistake in judging the industrial future of a country. In the 'eighties of the last century, the world viewed with scorn the cheap low-grade products which were 'made in Germany'. In time, however, this trade mark, at first a warning against the poor quality of the products, became a good advertisement for articles of particularly good quality. There is every indication that the label 'made in Japan' may also become an asset. Even to-day, in nearly all her industries, Japan is producing goods which prove her industrial ability. She needs only markets, at home and abroad, in order to develop her production more rapidly.

CHEAP EXPORT GOODS

The products on view in Japanese factories manufacturing for export, in export exhibitions, or in the displays of Japanese export merchants, are not as good quality as the articles sold in the department stores and the good shops in Tokyo, or as the goods used by members of the upper middle class. This is true both of the products of the old home industries and of the new large factories. Not only is the quality of the goods seen in factories or exhibitions poorer, but the standard of taste is often so low that it seems inconceivable that a people with such sure taste in their own national products could have designed some of these articles.

But having discussed elsewhere what Japan can achieve in quality, we shall now see what she can achieve in price. Her main idea is to supply the small consumer all over the world with commodities which hitherto he could not afford, and in which cheapness is the essential factor. At an incredibly low price the small consumer gets goods of practical as well as psychological value.

'I own one of those things, too ; it is just like the other fellow's, though he has so much more money than I have.' This idea, originating from an urgent need to find employment for Japanese workers, has been largely realized during the world economic crisis, which reduced purchasing power everywhere.

That this idea has been realized emerges clearly from the following figures taken from Japan's official export statistics for 1933. True, these figures represent averages which include many types and qualities of goods, but they convey a general impression better than could isolated examples.

Average prices of some Japanese export goods at the exchange rate of the time :

1 square yard of bleached shirting, 2½*d.* ; 1 square yard of printed jean, 2¾*d.* ; 1 square yard of bleached cotton flannel, 3⅓*d.* ; 1 dozen silk handkerchiefs, 2*s.* 4*d.* ; 1 dozen cotton handkerchiefs, 8¼*d.* ; 1 dozen white cotton shirts, stiffened, 7*s.* 3*d.* ; 1 dozen pair silk socks or stockings, 7*s.* 9*d.* ; 1 dozen pair other socks or stockings, 1*s.* 11*d.* ; 1 dozen pair rubber boots and shoes, 9*s.* 6*d.* ; 1 dozen Thermos bottles,

8*s*. 4*d*.; 1 dozen cutlery articles, 1*s*.; 1,000 sewing needles, 4*d*.; 1 dozen European umbrellas, 11*s*. 8*d*.; 1 electric lamp, ½*d*.; 1 dozen pencils, less than 1*d*.

The prices of bicycles manufactured for export are to-day from 7*s*. 6*d*. (for orders over 10,000) to 38*s*. The cheaper makes are quite good, the more expensive ones are of excellent quality.

This list does not by any means include all the commodities exported by Japan. Their number is increasing rapidly. The first cheap motor-cars entirely built in Japan have found buyers in the world-markets, and a large expansion is already planned. There is hardly a modern industrial commodity which Japan does not to-day produce, or at least plans to produce, for export.

HOW THEY COMPETE

Japan does not always export exactly the same articles as those exported by Western countries. Prices fluctuate greatly from day to day, and vary according to the export firm and according to the purchaser. A general comparison between Japanese export goods and those of other countries is therefore impossible. But the last few years have shown that Japanese goods, not only because they are specially suitable for the small consumer, but even where comparisons can be made, are considerably and often surprisingly cheaper than competitive goods made in other countries. A few examples chosen at random will illustrate this point:

A collection of Japanese goods was displayed in an exhibition organized by the Economic League in London early in 1934. The whole collection, ranging from textiles and chinaware to electrical goods and toys—goods, by the way, originating both from the 'old' and from the 'new' Japan—could have been sold on the English market for £3 14*s.* 5*d.* In England, however, the articles included in this display would have cost £12 or £14 to produce, that is to say about four times as much. Japanese shirts which, in Lancashire, were sold to the retail trade at £1 1*s.* a dozen, would cost at least £1 12*s.* to produce in Lancashire, that is to say about 50 per cent more—quite apart from the costs of packing, freight, insurance, and wholesaler's profit. The production cost of rubber beach balls, which are sold in England by Japanese exporters for from £1 1*s.* to £2 8*s.* per gross, would be twice or three times as high if these articles were manufactured in England. A case of mathematical instruments for architectural use, sold in the Tokyo retail trade for 8.50 yen, that is 10*s.* 3*d.*, was sent to London, and it was found that a comparable article cost between three and four guineas in a London shop. Up to a short time ago good-quality standard bleached shirting of Japanese manufacture cost exactly half as much in India as the English product of only slightly better quality. Such differences in price are also reported with regard to many other Japanese goods and comparable goods produced in England or other Western countries. The following example is particularly interesting:

One of the best-known makes of portable gramophones is manufactured in exactly the same model in Tokyo and in London. The difference in quality (if any) is somewhat in favour of the Japanese product, for which a higher standard for several of the metal parts is being specified. Despite the fact that the same discount is allowed the Tokyo retail trade, that the manufacturers' profit is at least as great, and that the working and wage conditions in this plant are far above the average Japanese standards, and not very much below the English, this gramophone is sold in Tokyo for 35 yen = £2 2*s*, whilst in London it costs £4. The most expensive model of this particular gramophone is made exactly alike in Japan and in the United States. In Tokyo it sells for 75 yen = $23.50, while in the United States it costs $50.00.

CHAPTER THREE

VISITING JAPANESE WORKERS

HOME-MADE COTTON CLOTH

IN a small industrial town, at the foot of a beautiful mountain range, a small wooden house stands among rice fields and mulberry groves. In the house six broad iron looms, of the usual size, are worked by electricity. The staff of this small home industry consists of the owner, his wife and the neighbour's child, and they are all very busy.

They begin work in the morning at six o'clock. Three times a day they rest: twice for fifteen minutes and once for thirty minutes. The machines are stopped in the evening at half-past six. Then next day's work is prepared; the woman cooks a meal and the man writes his letters. Twice a month they take a day off.

There is no door between the family's bed-sitting-room and the workshop where the looms are rattling. The floor of this room is somewhat raised and is covered with a mat. There is a low table, a few cushions and a small iron bowl to hold glowing charcoal. Beyond is the kitchen.

Each of the second-hand looms costs 90 yen (£5 8*s.*). They are sold in the village street just as elsewhere bicycles might be offered for sale. The man owns the looms, but he is 300 yen (£18) in debt. His creditor is either a merchant or a factory owner of whom he buys his yarn and to whom he sells his cloth. It is worth while remarking that there is a brisk market for second-hand looms, which lessens the financial burden of modernization.

The man and his wife earn about 110 yen a month (£6 12*s.*). The electricity they use, very cheaply generated by water power, costs them about 50 sen a day, that is 15 yen (18*s.*) a month. The neighbour's child is paid 40 yen (£2 8*s.*) a year, less than 1½*d.* a day. The taxes are not much more than 6 yen (7*s.* 2*d.*) a year.

The average daily production of this home industry is 300 yards of good cloth, woven in many-coloured patterns. Most of the orders received are for the export trade. Therefore this man is much better off than his neighbour who manufactures kimono material for home consumption. This neighbour uses ten narrow looms, which he has bought second-hand for 50 yen (£3) each. He, too, has debts amounting to 300 yen; and he, his wife and his brother work from six o'clock in the morning until seven o'clock in the evening. He has two small children to support and his total monthly income varies from 50 to 70 yen (£3–£4 4*s.*).

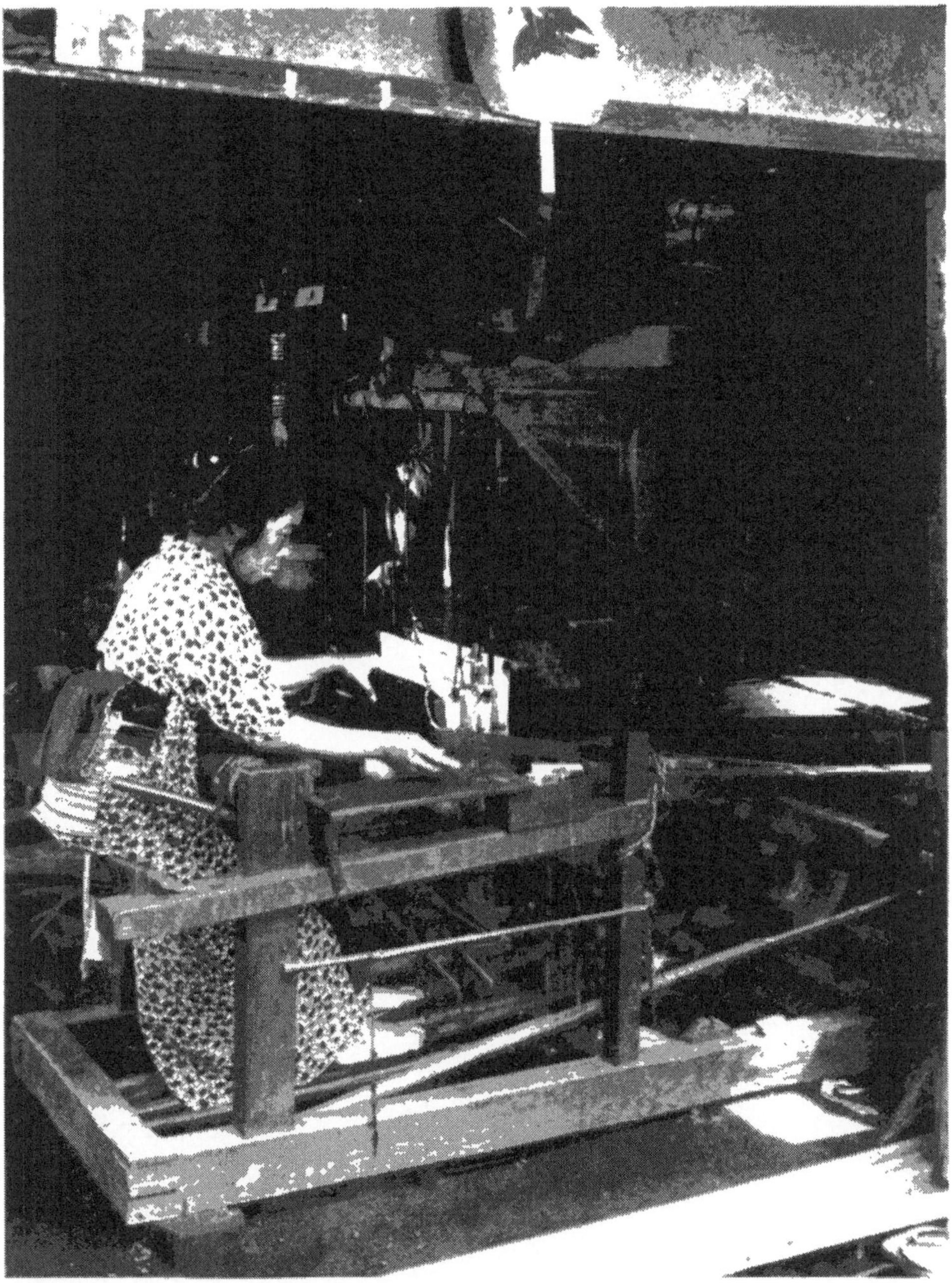

Home-made Cotton Cloth

A PENCIL COMBINE

In a small wooden house in a side road in Tokyo, behind a latticed sliding door, which serves as a window as well, a man, a woman and a young girl are seated on the clean, mat-covered floor. They bundle and label pencils, which are brought to them from a factory near their home. The pencils are tied together in neat little packages of twelve with gay pictures on top. The family work with quick, automatic movements.

They work from early in the morning until late at night, and when the small children come home from school they spend eight hours, so the mother says, helping the older members of the family bundle and pack. Each child earns 15 sen (2¼*d.*) for eight hours' work a day. The whole family, five people, earn on an average 50 to 60 yen a month (£3 to £3 12*s.*).

Forty families near the factory are employed in a similar manner. Before they get the pencils, many other families in Northern Japan, in Hokkaido, a district rich in wood and graphite, have worked under similar conditions making the unfinished pencils which are sent to the Tokyo factory in huge bundles.

The factory itself is merely a large handicraft plant laid out in thinly walled wooden workshops of somewhat improvised appearance. The machinery is more or less primitive. The forty men and women employed in this factory are mostly young and they earn between 15 and 30 yen a month (18*s.* and £1 16*s.*). Only the finishing of the pencils is done here: they are painted, polished and the name is printed on them. In all, the factory sees to the planning of the work of about a hundred small family enterprises, from the purchase of raw materials to the distribution of the finished pencils.

This combine produces 600,000 gross—86,400,000 pencils—a year. The cheaper ones are sold to the wholesale trade at prices ranging from 3 to 3.2 sen (.45*d.*) a dozen. Pencils with an india-rubber at the top are sold at 6.6 sen (.96*d.*) a dozen. The best quality cost 25 sen (3½*d.*) a dozen. None are of poor quality. This one factory, employing a hundred families and forty factory workers, exports its pencils to forty countries.

This 'pencil combine', and the cotton weaving home industry described earlier in this chapter, are typical of the first category of Japanese workshops, manufacturing in innumerable branches of industry for export and home consumption: small home enterprises, co-operating informally with the trade and with small-scale industries, and incorporated into a larger unit of production and distribution.

A BICYCLE FACTORY

In another narrow side road, so typically Japanese, there are a number of small primitive workshops, one story high, made of wood and corrugated iron. Three hundred boys and young men are standing on the uneven floors of these workshops in front of small iron foundries, at modern shaping, paring, cutting and polishing machines, at galvanizing tubs, at tables for assembling and packing, and benches at which many of the machines needed for the production of bicycles are made.

This factory produces one of the best makes of Japanese bicycles. Almost every part is manufactured on the spot, from the crudest raw material to the finished frame. Only the wheels and a few of the parts are bought outside from handicraft shops or modern factories. Two hundred of the men working in this factory are apprentices; 100 are regular workmen. They are all earnest, obviously intelligent, and concentrated on their work. They work from seven o'clock in the morning until five o'clock in the afternoon with an hour's rest at noon, and apart from the national holidays (among others a five days' holiday at New Year) they have two free days a month. At present, as a result of the flourishing export trade, they work three and a half hours' overtime daily.

The apprentices are paid on an average 35 yen (£2 2*s*.) a month. Of this, in common with the regular workmen, they pay 12*s*. a month for their food, which is served three times a day in a simple clean dining-room. They sleep in dormitories near the workshops. These are small wooden Japanese houses, the rooms bare of furniture save for the mats which cover the floors. Each boy is allowed two *tatami*, that is to say, twice the space needed by an outstretched man. The young men's belongings, and by day, the *futon*, or Japanese beds, are kept in cupboards along the walls.

The regular workmen, who live with their families, are paid 30 yen to 105 yen a month. The average wage is 60 yen (£3 12*s.*) a month —from which 12*s.* a month is deducted for food. Married men receive 6*s.* more. (As in Europe, 'outworkers' receive much less—an average monthly wage of 30 yen for ten hours' work a day (exclusive of meal times) is paid to an outworker making chains for a bicycle factory in Osaka). In addition, when trade is good, they receive a bonus of from £3 to £6 a year. A bonus of 6*s.* is paid when a member of their family dies; the same amount is paid at the birth of a child; a bonus of £3 is awarded when they marry, and when a workman dies his family is given £18. The workmen pay their insurance premiums themselves.

The owner of this factory, a highly intelligent self-made man, is the technical director, the works manager, and the father of the working 'family' all in one. No expert, no trades union, separates him from his workmen; the relationship between them is that which prevails in old handicraft plants. The foremen, half appointed and half elected, are the only supervisors in the plant. Their role is that of experienced crafts-

At the Toyo Spinning Company in Osaka

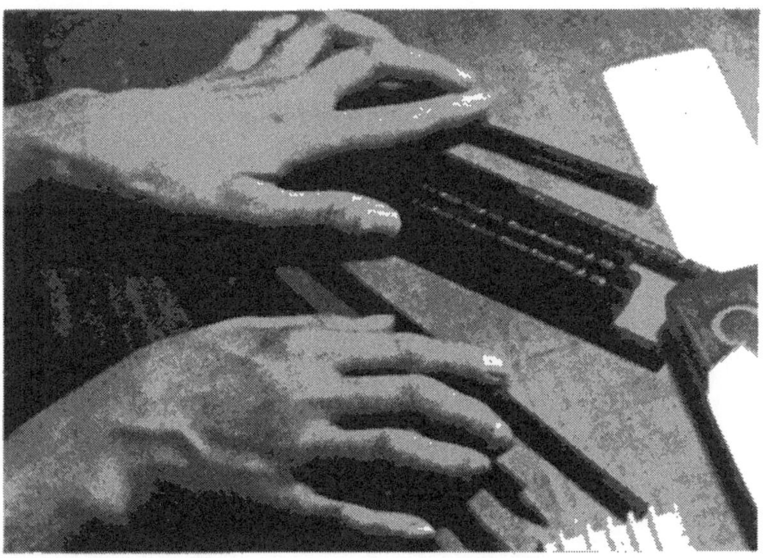

The hands that do it—Pencil Factory

men. Twenty of them, one from each department, form the works council. They wear a purple scarf round their heads, while the ordinary workmen wear red scarves, and the helpers wear yellow or blue ones.

A whistle goes and the twenty members of the works council stand in line in the courtyard between the workshops. The senior member calls out to them and they bow low three times before their master and his guest, just as Japanese sons bow before their father. The most efficient workmen wear bronze and silver medals, and at the front of the factory, in the modest office, there is a card index with their records and their photographs. Every month a note is made of the production of each worker, of their 'experience', their 'responsibility', their 'devotion', 'kindness', 'common sense', &c. To a certain extent their wages depend upon these records. (It might be mentioned that the owner has never been outside Japan.)

The wholesale price of the finished bicyles—about 200 are produced daily—is 30 yen (£1 16*s*.). This price is almost three times as high as that of the cheapest Japanese mass-production bicycles, but the former seem to be of really good quality.

This factory, which manufactures largely for the home market, has considerable export sales as well, and prints an attractive catalogue in English. It is typical of the second category of Japanese workshops manufacturing for export: super-handicraft establishments with modern machines, most of which are still served by hand. It is organized and managed according to patriarchal methods of handicraft tradition.

A PIONEER'S FACTORY

One day in 1909, the spiral gear of a British-made gas engine suddenly broke. Nobody in Japan could make a new one. The work was urgent. A short, modest little workman was found who succeeded, with his primitive tools, in copying the complicated mechanism which had been produced in England by the latest modern precision machines.

He still remains the modest little workman. He works from dawn to dusk in his gear-cutting plant which is the largest in Japan and probably one of the finest in the world. He wears a worker's blue overall ; his hands are oily. His three brothers are now working with him. Together they own their factory worth 3,000,000 yen, and employing 260 workers.

The chief and his three brothers do not take more pay from the factory than the highest-paid employee's 5.30 yen per day (6*s.* 6*d.* at present rates). The engineers just reach the average wage of the staff at 3.50 yen (4*s.* 3*d.*) per day. The profits, which are considerable, are invariably reinvested in the factory. The owner has never taken a day off, does not drink, smoke or gamble, but is happy and enthusiastic. From a special fund he allows himself an expense account not exceeding 200 yen (£12) per month, but he hardly ever touches it except for the education of his children. He says that he considers the factory not as his property but as a trust which he is called upon to administer. Money, he says, does not interest him, it does not even give him an incentive. What he really wants is to cut beautiful gears, and as far as he has any other interests, he is proud of being an example for many Japanese industrialists who, in his view, spend far too much, live far too well and work far too little! He served a hard apprenticeship with his father, and he maintains the patriarchal principle in his factory, though with high wages, an eight-hour day and two free Sundays a month.

This man is considered a technical genius—it is said that there is no gear in the world which he cannot reproduce accurately. And gears are, after all, vital to the engineering industry, to modern armaments, to shipbuilding, and many other industries.

Not only Japanese but even Western engineers bring their most complicated technical problems to this original genius who taught himself to work with logarithms and mechanical text-books, but who still relies more on his sight and touch.

A good deal of the progress of the Japanese engineering industry rests on the success of this small factory, which does nothing else but cut infinite varieties of gears from blue prints sent to them. According to authoritative British experts this factory represents one of the important pointers to the great future of Japanese industry.

Here is a German machine worth 360,000 yen. It is so tall that the main hall of the factory had to be raised to a height of 60 feet. It is said to be the best of its kind, and there are only eight of them in the world. This machine works entirely without any human assistance and with very little human supervision. At present it is grinding the teeth of a giant gear for a large ship. The price of this gear is 1,000 yen, and it takes three days and three nights of uninterrupted work to produce. In this way the machine is earning 30 per cent per annum of its capital cost without giving full-time work to a single man. The total expenses of this factory are said to be recovered from the sales of the metal waste.

The owner himself often builds new machines or adapts old ones for special orders. Only for the most complicated processes is he still a customer for British and other foreign machines ; in other fields he is already a successful competitor. The regular flood of orders for armaments and for export keep his machines working at capacity and afford him scope for unlimited expansion.

THE BIG COTTON MILLS

Large buildings surrounded by an outside wall. Long, rather low, light and well-ventilated workshops. Long flat-roofed friendly wooden dormitory houses for the factory girls who form nine-tenths of the staff. Open squares, gardens, playing fields, intersected by paved and often roofed-in paths. Self-sufficient little towns separated by walls from the large cities round them; with their own power station, spinning, weaving and auxiliary plants, with dwelling-houses, canteens, swimming baths, schools, theatres, hospitals and shops. The atmosphere is a mixture of boarding school and orphanage, super-factory and old-world handicraft shop. This is a picture of one of the 250 great Japanese cotton factories which have achieved first place in the cotton markets of the world.

It is even more difficult to inspect these factories than it is to visit other Japanese industrial plants (those of the heavy industries, chemical, rayon and engineering are altogether inaccessible). Technically they are by no means alike. In some of them, in spite of all rationalization, one sees only machines labelled 'Platt Bros. Ltd., Oldham 1907'. Nobody dreams of replacing these machines, for they are still working efficiently, and the mills using them are making large profits. In other factories again one sees only machines labelled 'Toyoda Loom Factory—Made in Japan' of very recent date. Often machines are mixed by both origin and date in still other mills—both English and Japanese machines are found working side by side. But whether machines are old or new experiments are always being made in labour-saving, greater speed and larger production. In one factory, which was so empty of operatives that the layman thought he had found a perfect illustration of rationalized plant, the chief engineer stated that current experiments would allow still further reduction of labour and a large increase of production after next year.

It is not unusual to find a single girl operating from 400 to 800 spindles. No trade union prevents her from handling as many as she is able. The piecework system, which rules almost throughout, stimulates them to the utmost. The movements of these girls make a deep impression upon the observer. They are somehow different from those seen in any Western country. They are different even when they are working on machines similar to those operating in Lancashire, the U.S.A., Germany or Russia. It is as if a typical Japanese element of feminine devotion and whole-heartedness transforms the work on spindles and looms, on packing and sorting tables, into a strange ceremonial service.

In one mill it was said that the girls reached the peak of their efficiency after two to two and a half years. In most cases efficiency decreased after that time. The reason for this curious phenomenon was not known. Most girls in this particular concern, which owns many factories in Japan, work only from twenty-five to thirty months, after which they return to their parents in the country.

The operatives in this factory are at present

Girls of a Cotton Mill Works having a lesson in flower arrangement and playing piano

between twenty and thirty years of age, but the younger girls predominate. There is always a long waiting list. The employment agents for the firm are spread over the whole country, and they co-operate with the local authorities in recruiting labour. There is at present keen competition between the rayon and cotton industries for new workers. The firm in question pays about the highest wages in the industry. The minimum daily rate is .40 yen—at present 5½*d.*—but the average wage is .91 yen—1*s.* 0½*d.* —of which .15 yen—2*d.*—is deducted for food. At these rates the firm need fear no competition. It need not even, as was formerly the case, make contracts with the parents of the girl. In some cases the girls will even pay their own fare from village to factory on which the State railways grant a 50-per-cent reduction. The custom of paying to the farmers cash advances on the wages of their daughters is no longer prevalent among firms of good reputation. No particular encouragement is needed nowadays to induce farmers to send their daughters into the factories.

Most cotton mills work in two shifts of eight and a half hours each. For seventeen hours a day all machines are working incessantly. That is another secret of modern Japanese production.

DORMITORY LIFE

In a Silk Factory.—One of the largest and most up-to-date Japanese silk factories has been built in a pleasant park outside the metropolis. In the long halls of this wooden factory hundreds of young girls stand before modern spinning looms, which are continuously being improved in the factory itself. The girls are small, and not all of them look strong. They wear short skirts—those of the supervisors are of a different colour—and white stockings. All are serious, concentrated upon their difficult task, and keep pace with the speed dictated by the machines. According to European reckoning only a few of the girls are over twenty and the youngest about fifteen. (According to Japanese custom a child is considered to be a year old on the day of its birth. On the following New Year's Day it is two.)

They are the children of peasants and most of them have come from the poorest districts of Japan. Their parents have made an agreement for a year with the company which owns the factory—the law no longer allows longer agreements—and this contract is renewed from year to year, usually over a period of three to five years.

They work from five o'clock in the morning until five o'clock in the afternoon with two hours' rest. The average daily wage is .70 yen (10$\frac{1}{4}$*d.*). A part of this wage is given to them as pocket money. They live rent free in the dormitories. Each girl is allowed the space which would be taken up by two mats and they keep the rooms, as well as their persons, scrupulously clean.

Three apparently decent meals are served free of charge in a sanitary dining-room, where they spend their time off duty laughing and talking loudly. They have bathrooms, a large recreation-room and a sanatorium. If they wish they can go into the village in the evening, but lights must be out by a quarter to nine. The relatively few men employed in this factory also sleep in dormitories.

Each girl spins on an average twelve skeins of raw silk a day from the cocoons raised by the farms in the district; that is about the quantity of silk needed to produce seventy-two pairs of average-sized women's stockings.

This factory manufactures almost exclusively for export. It is typical of a third category of Japanese workshops which includes almost the entire cotton industry and a few other textiles: technically super-modern, large-scale factories, highly rationalized, scientifically managed, company-owned and based socially on the dormitory system.

In a Cotton Mill.—Six young girls employed in the cotton-spinning plant already described sat opposite us on a bench in the dining-room. They wore attractive, colourful kimono, for it was their hour of rest. Half-laughing, half-serious, they answered questions about their life in the factory.

On that particular week they were working in the morning shift, and this was their day's programme: 4.30 a.m. getting up and washing in the bathroom; 5 a.m. work begins; 7.30 to 8 a.m. breakfast; 2 p.m. lunch, and then rest until 4 p.m.; from 4 p.m. to 6 p.m. school; 6 p.m. to 8 p.m. recreation, and 8 p.m. bed.

The night shift works from 2 until 11 p.m. Every Sunday is free and some of the girls go out. Most of them, however, stay for games in the factory compound. Few of them have relatives in the neighbourhood, for they are all country girls, and most of them come from a considerable distance.

They earn from .40 to 1.50 yen a day, according to the length of time they have been employed in the factory, the type of work they do and their efficiency. Piece rates are paid in almost all of the departments. The average wage is .80 yen a day (1*s.* 7½*d.* at par; 11½*d.* at present rates). The girls pay the factory .13 yen a day for their board and keep. Full board actually costs .10 yen a day more, but the management contributes this amount. The average net wage, therefore, amounts to .67 yen a day. The girls are paid 3 to 5 yen pocket money on the twenty-eighth of every month. The rest of the money is usually sent to their homes, where, if they are fortunate, some of it is saved. If not, the girls' wages help to support their families, and these subsidies are an important form of farm relief.

The girls like being in the factory, where work is less arduous than it would be in the rice fields, in silkworm sheds, in a household, or at home taking care of their younger brothers and sisters.

Weaving of Kimono Cloth

The food provided is good and usually plentiful. A scientific laboratory supervises their diet. Rationalization in this factory has caused the staff to be halved during the last five years, so that the girls have more room in their dormitories than they ever had at home, not to speak of the playing fields and the common-room with its occasional cinema shows and amateur theatrical performances. Nor did they have pocket money at home, and here they can save money or help support their families, or both. In the factory, furthermore, they have at least as much freedom as they had in their patriarchal homes, where women and girls are not considered important. They also attend a 'junior grade high school', not usually open to peasant girls.

These girls are honest and childlike enough not to pretend that work is what they like best in dormitory life. Instead, with shining eyes, they told us that they like school best. In view of the Japanese passion for learning this answer is very understandable. In the attractive schoolrooms where, for two hours every day, they sit attentive on their mats, they are taught the usual subjects, including lessons in deportment and ceremonial customs: how to bow and to walk properly, how to kneel and serve tea, how to arrange flowers according to Japanese tradition. It is a pretty sight to see the girls, in rows of six, facing each other and bowing low in the prescribed rhythm.

Undoubtedly these girls are among the more

fortunate Japanese workers, and as they can compare life in the factory with the miserable conditions in their homes, they are obviously content.

AN ENTIRELY MODERN FACTORY

In a modern industrial district there is a new three-storied factory building of stone, with large light workrooms in which hundreds of workmen stand in front of machines. Almost all of these workers are men over twenty years of age, and many of them are highly skilled.

They produce one of the best types of Japanese fountain-pens from the semi-raw material to the beautifully packed finished product. The employees work eight hours a day ; they have four days off a month ; they are all independent and live in their own homes. The lowest wage paid is 35 yen (£2 2*s*.), the highest is 140 yen (£8 8*s*.), and the average is between £4 4*s*. and £4 16*s*. a month. The company observes the rules of the trades union to which all workers must belong.

The company considers the workmen as officials. As a result wages are paid monthly. One custom from patriarchal days, still important throughout Japanese industry, is observed here: a dismissal fee is paid when workers are discharged. This amounts, for instance, to the equivalent of forty-five days' wages when the man has been employed in the factory for two years; of one hundred and sixty days after five years; five hundred and fifteen days after twenty years. It should be mentioned that the manager of this factory believes that, managed on the social system prevailing in his factory, Japanese industry would retain its competitive ability, and he is as satisfied with the development of his company's export trade as are the managers of most of the other factories we visited.

This factory produces 300,000 gold-nibbed fountain-pens a month. Their retail prices vary from 2 to 80 yen each. Some of them are simple pens, others are made with gold inlay lacquer work of traditional Japanese design. These elaborate pens are used by Japanese diplomats when they sign international agreements.

This factory, too, manufactures partly for export. It is typical of those modern Japanese works which most closely resemble Western factories, and which produce goods of excellent quality.

CHAPTER FOUR

THE STRUCTURE OF JAPANESE INDUSTRY

PRINCIPAL TYPES OF ORGANIZATION

THE export goods labelled 'Made in Japan' come from every type of organization: from small family industries and small or medium-sized handicraft units, more or less linked up with family enterprises; from super-handicraft plants, representing the greater part of medium-sized industry; from large factories based on peculiarly Japanese semi-feudal social organization; from similar factories organized on Western lines. All these types of plants play an important part in Japanese production and export trade.

It is not possible to state the relative importance of each type of plant. A general analysis of Japanese industry can only be made on the basis of the *size* of various units, which corresponds only roughly to the classes described above because these were regarded more from the point of view of their technical and social organization than from the point of view of the number of workers employed. In particular, the following analysis by size cannot differentiate between the 'semi-feudal' and the 'Western' types of large factories.

Very small units, employing less than five persons, are not included in the Japanese Factory Statistics. These small workshops still have an important share in the total industrial production. According to the Chamber of Commerce in Tokyo, they produced in 1931 18·8 per cent of the total output of cotton textiles; 28·8 per cent of woollen textiles; 55·1 per cent of silk textiles; 27·4 per cent of hosiery goods; 29·1 per cent of hats; 91·5 per cent of pencils; 60·8 per cent of china ware; 65·5 per cent of bicycles (assembling as well as production of parts). It is possible that since 1931 these percentages have declined somewhat, though not very much, for these small home enterprises have become increasingly important to various industries, including the manufacture of toys, wooden products, basket ware, brushes, dressmaking, and the production of parts for larger works. Ten per cent is therefore probably a low estimate of the output of these very small workshops in relation to the total value of Japan's industrial production.

In 1932, the last year for which a census was compiled, 13 per cent of all registered workers were in small industrial establishments employing from 5 to 9 persons—the smallest units included in the Japanese Factory Statistics.

Twenty-six per cent of all workers were employed in workshops with from 10 to 49 employees. In view of their organization these establishments must also be included amongst the smaller industries. Altogether, therefore, small industries employ about 39 per cent of Japan's industrial workers.

Medium-sized industries, as we shall arbitrarily call those plants employing from 50 to 500 workers, absorb a further 36 per cent of Japan's industrial labour.

This means that in the large factories, employing 500 workers or more, only 25 per cent of Japanese workers are employed.

With regard to the value of annual output, a rough estimate, taking into account the foregoing facts about the 'dwarf units', shows the following relation between the four categories of industrial establishments:

The smallest industries	at least	10 per cent
Small industries	,,	29 per cent
Medium-sized industries	,,	35 per cent
Large industries	,,	26 per cent

Or to put it differently: one-half of Japan's total production is manufactured in workshops employing less than 75 workers, while the other half is produced in factories employing more than 75 workers. This shows that Japan is still substantially a country of small industries.

This fact must not be forgotten in any investigation of her export trade, just as it must be remembered that the semi-feudal character of the old family system continues to affect her entire industrial development. The third important fact, emerging from a study of the structure of Japanese industry, is that gradually she is ceasing to be a textile producing country only.

Twenty-five years ago textiles represented half of Japan's total output as far as it was recorded in her statistics; in 1914 they amounted to 45 per cent. In 1932, however, they were only 37 per cent, despite the tremendous development of the textile industry itself. For other industries have grown even more rapidly, and though to-day textiles still head the list, the metal and machinery industries, which were relatively insignificant before the World War, now follow closely with almost 20 per cent, and chemicals with 16 per cent of Japan's total production. Together, therefore, these two industries are now as important to Japan's total production as is the textile industry.

Japan continues, however, to be largely a country of 'light' industries producing goods for consumption—a country in which the heavy industries, which produce capital goods, are relegated to second place because of her shortage of raw materials. But Japan is continually expanding her production of machinery, instruments, and metal goods of all kinds, products which depend on supplies from foreign heavy industries. And with the help of these products and of her own growing chemical industry she is gradually increasing her output of the great variety of finished products mentioned in the last chapter. Other branches of Japanese industry, therefore, are not affected by the slow development of her own heavy industries.

No branch of Japanese industry—artificial silk excepted—consists of large factories only. No branch of Japanese industry—with the possible exceptions of the wood and basket industries—consists of small factories only. In all branches of industry, workshops of all sizes, from 'dwarf' units to the largest factories, participate at least in an auxiliary character.

Large factories employing over 500 workers are most prominent in the textile industry, but even there they represent only 45 per cent of the industry as a whole; 39 per cent of the total textile output comes from medium-sized factories and 16 per cent from small workshops. We have mentioned the importance of the small family industries even in the most concentrated branch of the textiles group, the cotton industry.

Only 34 per cent of the machinery manufactured in Japan is produced in large factories. Forty-five per cent comes from medium-sized and 17 per cent from small establishments. Conditions in the metal industry are similar.

Only 21 per cent of Japanese chemicals are manufactured in large factories; 62 per cent are made in medium-sized factories.

The 'miscellaneous industries', manufacturing the inexpensive mass-production export goods which have recently caused so much uneasiness on world markets, produce only

12 per cent of their output in large, 52 per cent in medium-sized, and 36 per cent in small factories.

It is rarely possible to tell in what kind of a factory export goods, or their parts, have been manufactured. It is certain that most groups of exports are produced in all types of factories, though the percentage may vary from year to year and from market to market.

WHY SMALL-SCALE INDUSTRIES SURVIVE

In the West we have watched home industries and small-scale industries disappear when they clashed with modern industrial methods and modern social and political developments. This has not happened in Japan despite her rapid industrialization. On the contrary, though they have lost much of their traditional spinning and weaving work to larger and more modern factories, the textile industry remains practically the only really large-scale industry in Japan; but every year the older industrial establishments have begun to produce new articles. The total number of small-scale industries has increased by half since 1924.

There are many reasons for this development. The chief impulse behind it is the chronic depression of agriculture, the chronic over-population everywhere. These grim phenomena, which will be discussed in detail later, supply the small workshops with all the workers they need, often at a subsistence wage.

Japanese factory legislation allows small industries to exploit this situation more fully than is possible for the more efficient medium-sized and large industries, because the most important law affecting the hours of work—the law restricting them to ten hours a day, including one hour of rest, for women and children—is, as a rule, applied only to workshops employing ten workers or more. According to official records, 21 per cent of the workers included in statistical reports do not come under the factory law, and these statistics do not include the workers employed in small workshops employing less than five persons. Another law providing that factory regulations incorporating important protective measures for the workers must be drawn up and observed, applies only to factories employing more than fifty workers. Labour conditions in the small workshops are still based on the authoritative and patriarchal family system which favours the employer.

The widespread electrification of the country, based mainly on water power, supplies small enterprises with cheap power such as they could not afford in pre-electricity times. As far as power is concerned, the small industries now enjoy practically the same advantages as their larger competitors.

Even the smallest workshops can thus instal simple machines and motors, which are increasingly manufactured in the country, as well as water-wheels, the use of which has doubled during the last twenty years. Small industries also have less overhead charges than the larger factories.

Better transport facilitates the distribution of raw materials and finished products as well as the division of labour. The home and small-scale industries are encroaching on the production of various parts of high-class manufactures.

Some of the capital needed by family enterprises and small-scale industries comes from co-operative societies, but more comes from capitalists who are interested in their work either as manufacturers or as traders. Often these capitalists exert great pressure on the small manufacturers; in any case they pass on to them the pressure exerted on themselves by the competitive export trade.

The smallest factories in Japan, therefore, and the most primitive home industries thus become a part of the highly developed capitalist system, and the workers in the small workshop are indirectly employed by a vast industrial combine. Often small enterprises are virtually nothing but sub-departments or the employees of these combines. In the West the development was on different lines because the struggle between modern industry and the home industries began long before the introduction of cheap machine tools, easy transport or electricity, and long after the decline of the feudal system—at a time when agricultural conditions were not so bad as they are now, and when over-population was still relieved by emigration.

THE CONSEQUENCES OF RATIONALIZATION

It is not always easy for large Japanese factories to compete successfully with the small and less-efficient workshops, the owners of which are concerned less with profits than with the support of their families, or their family-like communities. The latter are forced by the threat of poverty to accept longer hours of work and lower wages, and their overhead charges and taxes are smaller than those of the larger industries.

These facts indicate that increased rationalization, especially in the textile industry, was caused not only by the international economic crisis and a desire for greater profits, but that Japanese industrialists also feared the competition of the small workshops at home. Rationalization has in fact been more highly developed in some of the large Japanese factories than it has in many Western countries. But rationalization means displacement of labour through the mechanization of production. The Japanese cotton industry is a good example of its effects. From 1924 to 1933 the sixty largest cotton factories, which practically control the modern section of the industry, doubled their production of yarn. The output of cotton cloth was increased by two-thirds. Employment did not increase. On the contrary, by means of rationalization, labour was decreased by 16 per cent, that is to say, it dropped to the level of 1919.

Despite the resilience of the small workshops with their low subsistence level, innumerable home and small-scale spinning and weaving plants have either been ruined or forced to change over to other industries. This means that employment in the Japanese cotton industry since the tremendous rise in the industry's international importance has decreased even more sharply than would appear from the official statistics. From 1924 to 1932, the last year for which figures are available, the number of persons working in spinning, twisting and cotton textile mills employing more than five persons dropped from 358,000 to 260,000, that is to say by 27 per cent. Again the decline would be much greater if the smallest workshops were included in these statistics.

It is probable that a similar decline would occur in any industry which was forced by competition with small and less efficient workshops to mechanize its large factories. The rationalization of the Japanese cotton industry has been chiefly responsible for the recent expansion of the range of goods produced by the home and small-scale industries. As the domestic demand for these new goods has been small, they have made great inroads on foreign markets. Indirectly, therefore, the modern cotton industry, which has ruined the small workshops as manufacturers and exporters of cotton textiles, has turned them into manufacturers and exporters of other articles.

What will happen when this development, which has been financially successful in the cotton industry, is repeated in other branches? when this development gradually limits the small workshops once more to a narrow field of production? If, for instance, the owner of the pencil 'combine' mentioned above realizes his intentions of manufacturing in one centralized and highly mechanized factory, a few of the families now working for him in their homes may be employed in the new plant, but the majority will be robbed of their home labour just as, not so long ago, they were deprived of their traditional spinning and weaving employment.

During recent years rationalization has by no means been confined to the cotton industry. Growing competition on foreign and domestic markets has forced most Japanese industries to rationalize their factories. This is illustrated by the fact that although from 1924 to 1932 the total output of industry, as well as the volume of exports, have doubled, 50,000 fewer persons were employed at the end of 1932 than eight years before. From 1932 to 1934, while production index rose 52 per cent, the index of employment rose only by 27 per cent.

Before we try to estimate the future of this

development, we must consider the importance of Japan's population problem.

THE POPULATION PROBLEM

Japan suffers from chronic over-population. This fact is not reflected in huge unemployment figures, because the traditional family system has always caused the members of a family to share their employment and their incomes as a matter of course. The system resembles the methods recently discussed and partially introduced in Western countries to alleviate acute unemployment.

In Japan, the family and not the State assumes the moral and material responsibility for the unemployed. True, to a certain extent the employer shares this responsibility, for though he pays no unemployment insurance premium, he grants the 'dismissal fees'. This custom, which has never been legalized, is not, however, a preventive measure against dismissal, and it is only of temporary help to the worker displaced by the machine.

Actually, almost every private agricultural enterprise, every small workshop and every retail business is 'over-populated', and only the larger establishments, which are entirely divorced from the family system and produce primarily for profit, are not over-staffed. Moreover, the population of Japan is increasing by about a million persons a year. This rise is due not only to the high birth rate, but also to a falling death rate.

Even if birth-control were rigidly observed, and this is at present inconceivable in Japan, employment conditions would not improve for a long time. Ten million workers, who will be on the labour market in ten or fifteen years, have already been born and many of them are growing up in better health and with better education than was possible for past generations of workers. They will doubtless make their demand for employment felt, both in domestic and foreign policies.

Agriculture cannot absorb them, for already many uneconomic plots are being cultivated. On the contrary, a reform of agriculture, so urgently needed, would cause a tremendous increase in unemployment amongst rural labour. Japanese workers, furthermore, have neither the desire nor the opportunity to emigrate. If, therefore, Japan wants to avoid a social catastrophe, she must provide industrial employment for her population, including the additional 10,000,000—5,000,000 of which are men—who will be needing work during the next few years. And, apart from these, she must consider the many millions who, to-day, are virtually in need of work, and those who, as rationalization progresses from year to year, are being thrown on to the labour market.

At present, after the developments and successes which have taken decades to achieve, after

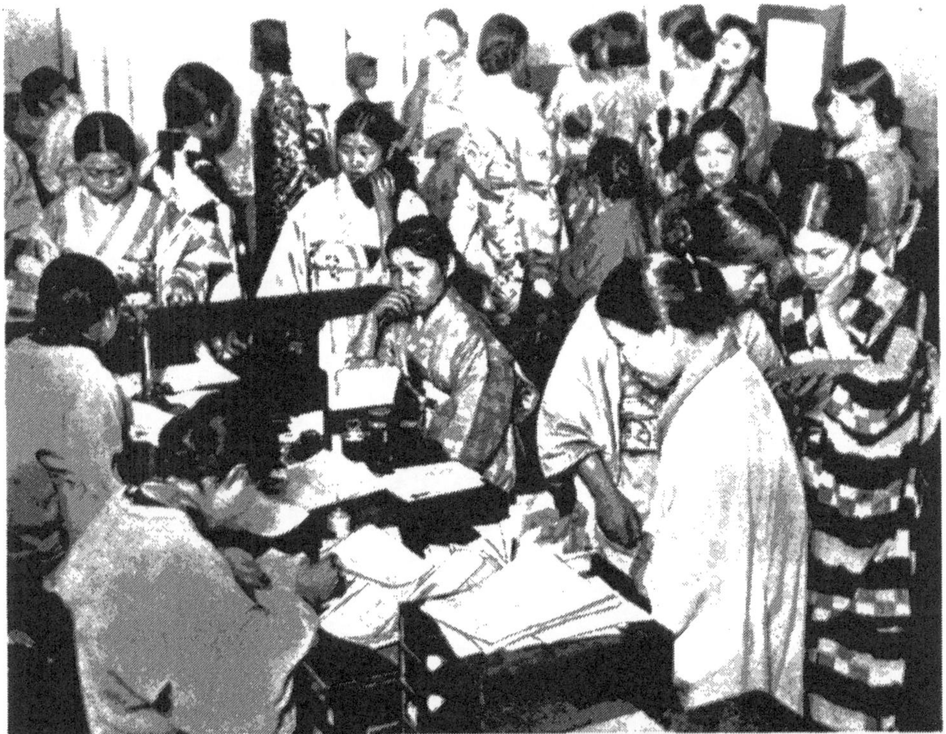

1. Girls at Osaka Central Labour Exchange
to take examination for service in Departmental Store

2. Unemployed men registering at Labour Exchange

immense investments of capital, after capturing extensive foreign markets, Japan is using only 2,000,000 regular industrial workers to produce her entire output of manufactured goods.

If Government-owned factories and public utilities are included, she now employs two and a half million. The large army of casual workers, however, who will be discussed later, are not included in the Factory Statistics. Excluding employment in the small home industries and workshops, it can be said that to-day, those Japanese industries in which the bulk of her financial resources are invested, and which are working more or less to capacity, are employing only two and a half million persons.

In theory, therefore, Japan must expand her industrial production by two-fifths every year merely in order to maintain the present state of employment, and to absorb the natural increase of her population. She should give up further rationalization and her large industries should not be developed more rapidly than her small workshops. For as the Factory Statistics indicate, workshops employing from five to nine persons must attain a net-production (and sale) averaging 2,500 yen a year to employ one worker, while in plants employing 200 workers, 4,000 yen worth of goods must be sold to make the employment of one worker economically possible.

As it is unlikely that either the capital or the domestic and foreign markets of Japan can be expanded quickly enough to keep pace with the increasing population ; as rationalization, furthermore, follows its own laws and cannot easily be stopped, it is probable that in the future the social struggle in Japan will become even more acute than it is to-day. In February 1935 three of the twelve Labour Exchanges of Osaka, Japan's most prosperous city, stated that they could find jobs for only 20 of the 300 men registering daily, and for 10 out of the 80 women. The total figures for unemployment in 1934 were officially stated as 380,000.

WAGES AND HOURS

This fact must be borne in mind when Japan's present and future wage policy is considered. In view of the great number of unemployed who would be willing to work in the factories for almost any wage, it is surprising not that wages are as low as they are in Japan, but that they are not lower.

In May 1934 the Imperial Cabinet published the following statistics of the average daily wages paid in 954 plants (including all bonuses and other cash extras paid) :

Silk reeling, 43.3 sen (6*d.*) ; baskets, 46.1 sen (6½*d.*) ; cotton spinning, 75.5 sen (11*d.*) ; silk textiles, 75.7 sen (11*d.*) ; knitted goods, 76.8 sen (11*d.*) ; twisting thread, 76.9 sen (11¼*d.*) ; buttons, 77.3 sen (11¼*d.*) ; cotton textiles, 78.5 sen (11½*d.*) ; matches, 78.7 sen (11½*d.*) ; flax textiles, 93.6 sen

(1*s.* 1½*d.*); hosiery, 96.0 sen (1*s.* 2*d.*); artsilk making, 104.3 sen (1*s.* 3*d.*); woollen textiles, 105.0 sen (1*s.* 3*d.*); flax spinning, 105.4 sen (1*s.* 3*d.*); shirt making, 106.1 sen (1*s.* 3¼*d.*); celluloid goods, 116.9 sen (1*s.* 5*d.*); soap and toilet goods, 119.3 sen (1*s.* 5*d.*); canning, 124.0 sen (1*s.* 6*d.*); woollen spinning, 124.9 sen (1*s.* 6*d.*); dyeing and bleaching, 131.3 sen (1*s.* 7*d.*); silk weaving, 134.3 sen (1*s.* 7½*d.*); stationery 149.5 sen (1*s.* 9½*d.*); watch making, 165.6 sen (2*s.*); sports goods, 177.6 sen (2*s.* 2*d.*); mining, 180.6 sen (2*s.* 2*d.*); shoes, 186.7 sen (2*s.* 3*d.*); agricultural implements, 190.4 sen (2*s.* 3½*d.*); rubber goods, 199.6 sen (2*s.* 5*d.*); enamel ware, 200.1 sen (2*s.* 5*d.*); bicycles, 207.0 sen (2*s.* 6*d.*); musical instruments, 207.6 sen (2*s.* 6*d.*); cement, 208.9 sen (2*s.* 6*d.*); beer brewing, 217.1 sen (2*s.* 7½*d.*); surgical instruments, 241.6 sen (2*s.* 11*d.*); linoleum, 242.0 sen (2*s.* 11*d.*); electric motors, 257.1 sen (3*s.* 1*d.*); spinning machinery, 264.7 sen (3*s.* 2*d.*); electric bulbs, 264.9 sen (3*s.* 2*d.*); munition and submarine, 266.6 sen (3*s.* 2½*d.*); cable and wires, 276.7 sen (3*s.* 4*d.*); motors and generators, 311.0 sen (3*s.* 9*d.*); motor-cars and cycles, 416.4 sen (5*s.*).

The preceding figures include cash bonuses but exclude 'indirect labour costs'. These are allowances for food and houses, expenses for sport and recreation, education, &c., particularly for living-in workers. Investigations by official authorities reveal that these costs, in the average of the whole Japanese industry, are less than 10 per cent, and probably not much more than 5 per cent of the total wage bill. They are naturally the highest in the dormitory factories of the textile industry.

It should be remembered that there is no insurance either for unemployment or for old age in Japan.

The daily wages listed in this table are based on a working day of slightly over 10 hours. On an average, ·57 hours of rest are allowed daily in a 27·4 days month.

The Tokyo *Far Eastern Social Information* of September 1, 1934, wrote as follows about the hours of work:

> The hours of work in large-scale weaving factories coming under the Factory Act are 11, including one hour for rest. 15 or even 16 hours are often worked in small-scale factories outside of the scope of the Factory Act or in those in the nature of handicraft or home industries. Two rest days per month are usually given in these factories. . . . Ten hours are generally worked in most factories employing 10 or more persons and engaged in the manufacture of articles of general merchandise, and 2 or 3 extra hours in time of pressure. Handicraft and home workshops not coming under the Factory Act usually work longer hours, often more than 12. No system of regular rest days exists in these workshops.

The Factory Statistics for 1932 include wage figures for all plants and workshops employing more than five persons in a few branches of industry. According to the Bank of Japan's Index wages from the end of 1931 to the autumn of 1934 fell by 8 per cent. The total

A typical urban retail shop for Japanese foot-gear
'Tabi' in the foreground

wage bill rose by 1·7 per cent, though there were 27 per cent more people employed at the end of the period. The 1932 figures can therefore be accepted as the maximum wages now paid in the various industries. The average hourly wage in 1932 was as follows in the industries listed :

Cotton spinning, 9 sen (1*s.* 3*d.*); cotton doubling, 8 sen (1*s.* 2*d.*); silk spinning, 8 sen (1*s.* 2*d.*); silk doubling, 6 sen (9*d.*); cotton weaving, 7 sen (1*s.*); cotton-silk mixed weaving, 6 sen (9*d.*); wool mixed weaving, 10 sen (1*s.* 5*d.*); rayon mixed weaving, 6 sen (9*d.*); knitted goods, 10 sen (1*s.* 5*d.*); dyeing, finishing, &c., 13 sen (1*s.* 9*d.*); porcelain and *cloisonné* manufacturing, 12 sen (1*s.* 9*d.*); sheet glass and glass ware, 16 sen (2*s.* 3*d.*); enamelled ironware manufacturing, 18 sen (2*s.* 6*d.*); celluloid articles, 12 sen (1*s.* 7*d.*); food preserving, 9 sen (1*s.* 3*d.*); umbrella manufacturing, 15 sen (2*s.* 2*d.*).

The latest wage figures published by the Bank of Japan are for the average daily earnings of workers in a comprehensive number of industries for October 1934. They were 1.34 yen for men and .68 yen for women (who comprise exactly one-half of Japan's industrial workers). As a contrast we quote a table published in 1934 by the American Steamship Owners Association which was much commented on in the Japanese Press. Although it refers not to industrial workers but to 'able seamen', it serves as a useful general comparison. The figures quoted are in American dollars. The Dutch mercantile marine paid the highest wages, $56.06 per month. Then comes the U.S.A., $52; Great Britain, $40.08; Germany, $39.21; France, $37.29; Norway, $36.57; Greece, $23.64, and Japan bringing up the rear with $11.68.

We quote these wages here only as cost factors included in the total production costs of finished products. It would be wrong to compare them with the wages of workers in other countries with different costs of living. The next chapter will describe what these wage costs really mean to the Japanese worker, and will compare their purchasing power with that of wages in Western countries. But even as a part of total production costs, the wages listed above must be modified before comparison with similar items in Western costing sheets; the productivity of the Japanese worker, that is to say, the effective value of an hour's work, or a day's work, must be estimated.

THE PRODUCTIVITY OF THE JAPANESE WORKMAN

Colin Clark, the English statistician who has compared the average productivity of Japanese and British workers, comes to the following conclusion:

> The Japanese worker has already reached 90% of the British productivity with his present working week. If the length of the working week were the same in the

two countries his productivity would not be more than 66% of the British. For a productivity per annum of 90% of the British level he receives an annual wage of 38% the British wage.

Experience shows that these estimates were correct when they were made (1930 for England; 1932 for Japan). In the meantime, however, increasing rationalization has probably equalized the average productivity of the workers in both countries, and Japan, of course, continues to make up for her disadvantages by longer hours of work. An average figure does not show, furthermore, that in the cotton industry, and perhaps in other industries as well, the productivity of the Japanese worker (or rather of the Japanese machine) is already greater than that of the English worker—even if the working hour and not the working day is used as a basis of comparison!

This development continues, not only as rationalization spreads to an increasing number of industries, but also as the Japanese worker becomes more experienced in his relatively new task. Technical and general schools in Japan are excellent, and we have already discussed the traditional skill of the Japanese. They are eager to learn, industrious and persistent, and existing industrial organization and customs in Japan give full scope to the ability of her workers. The legend of the industrial inferiority of the Asiatic races, at least as far as Japan is concerned, has been destroyed by reality.

We can assume that in the industries entering into international competition the productivity of the Japanese worker in relation to his weekly, though perhaps not his hourly wage, is not now very different from the productivity of the workers in the Western countries.

CAPITAL AND LABOUR

In the small workshops and the home industries no real differences exist between capital and labour. The owner of a small workshop, being virtually an employee of a larger firm, is at once both worker and capitalist. He is the father of the family and as such he is the master, for in his home the patriarchal attitude, strengthened by a very old feudal system, is still unweakened. And no class difference exists between this master and his economically stronger creditors, suppliers or customers. Between them there is merely the same difference which, in Western countries, separates the small and the large producer, the dependent and the controlling enterprises.

The semi-feudal, patriarchal traditions of the family system have, as we have seen, been preserved or modernized by other sections of Japanese industry—to the advantage of the workers as well as of the employers. The schools, the Press and the Government encourage these traditions as much as possible. All left-wing movements are considered unpatriotic in Japan and they have not been able to make themselves felt. The Trades Unions, at first inclining towards radicalism, achieved a slight success, but are now unimportant. The Trades Union Movement is still in that early stage indicated by the recent demand of the Japanese Trades Union Congress for 'legal recognition of freedom of association by the enactment of trade union legislation'. Still, the same Congress had sufficient 'freedom' to declare that 'the exceedingly inferior labour conditions existing in Japan, as compared with those in European and American countries, constitute one of the most important reasons for the rapid development of Japanese trade'.

Many Japanese trades unions have been organized, but their total membership is less than half a million. They have become a part of the national patriotic service, and they are governed by the wish to co-operate peacefully with the employers. As a result the unions present no difficulties whatsoever to the output of industry. Occasionally there have been strikes (in 1933 there were 1,880 disputes, during which 380,000 working days were lost), but the mass of unemployed, always ready to replace the strikers, make most strikes hopeless from the very beginning. The only gain to be derived by the workers from such an action is that occasionally the Government, which enjoys wide powers of arbitration, considering it to be a symptom of social unrest, decides in favour of the strikers.

Japan has not experienced the great industrial struggles which have played such an important role in Western countries, because in Japan industry is so differently organized. Labour conditions in agriculture are much worse than they are in industry; all Japanese Governments are patriarchal and conservative; and family traditions are still relatively strong.

All these factors have helped Japanese industry to avoid expensive social responsibilities which are now taken for granted in the West.

RULES OF A BICYCLE FACTORY

To illustrate the spirit prevailing in Japanese industry we are adding a few passages from the Factory Rules published by the bicycle factory mentioned above:

Song of the One Heart Band (Ishindan),
X.Y.Z. Bicycle Factory.[1]

However overwhelmingly the waves of the world's seas
May come on like flooding tides,
The One Heart Band'll rouse itself, sturdy as a rock,
With its iron arms of co-operation.

With the power of righteousness and the heart of chivalry,
Helping the weak and holding the strong,
Our brotherhood goes even through fire and water,
Of which the One Heart Band is proud before the world.

Looking forward to a Utopia of co-existence
Where our noble ideal is attainable,
Lo! the One Heart Band'll shine for ever
Gloriously with its glaring zeal.

. . . .

[1] Literal translation from the Japanese.

Then follows 'The General Plan of the X.Y.Z. Concern':

We, with a view to assisting national industrialization, shall try to develop social enterprises by the brotherhood organization of the working masses.

We, with a view to promoting the interests of the consumers at large, shall primarily aim at establishing a most rationalized system of producing and distributing bicycles.

We shall try fully to protect the interests of each member of our concern and secure him or her an appropriate means of living.

We, with a view to promoting the common interest of our factory, distributing stations and agents, shall try to realize the unification of the whole enterprise as one and the same heart and body.

Each member shall try intently to promote the interest of all members and shall never forget the demands of the whole body. No member shall do anything against the interest of the whole.

We, with a view to continuously strengthening the position of all members, shall aim at establishing a rational system of (consumers' or employees'?) credit as early as possible.

. . . .

Next come the works rules, at first for apprentices:

Qualification for Employment: Age—15 to 17. Education: Graduates from the higher primary school course who have passed the entrance examination of the management. Work: The Factory Laws shall be applied, while the private regulations of this factory shall be observed when necessary. Apprenticeship: Any employee shall be an apprentice until he is fully 21 years old. Those who begin work after that age shall remain apprentices for the next four years of their employment.

The monthly pay for apprentices is fixed as follows:

First grade, 20 yen; second grade, 18 yen; third grade, 16 yen; fourth grade, 14 yen; fifth grade, 12 yen; sixth grade, 10 yen; seventh grade, 8 yen; eighth grade, 7 yen; ninth grade, 6 yen; tenth grade, 5 yen; probatory grade, 4 yen. Every apprentice shall be on probation for one year of employment.

Apprentices get the following allowances in kind: Food (estimated at about 35 sen a day); bedding to be lent free of charge. Each apprentice shall be supplied with soap. Dwelling quarters are free. Twenty-five bath tickets a month will be given to each apprentice. Health insurance fee will be paid by the management.

The bonus system for apprentices is regulated as follows:

(*a*) Reward for Regular Attendance. Every apprentice who attends all the working days of the month will get one yen. (*b*) Periodic Bonuses.—(1) At the end of the first half of the company's business year, every apprentice who has served for more than six months will get a bonus of 10 yen; those who have served longer will get an additional reward of one yen for every six months' service. Those who attended every work-day in the first half of the year will get a special reward of 8 yen. In connexion with the last reward, each case of part-time absence by attending too late or leaving too early will decrease the sum by 50 sen and each case of a full day's absence by 1 yen. (2) At the end of the year, the general reward of 15 yen, the long-service reward of 1.50 yen for every six months' service, and the full-attendance reward of 8 yen will be given to every qualified apprentice. Every apprentice who reaches the conscriptional age during his employment will get 25 yen for each year after the probation.

Absence is permitted, for instance,

When the apprentice's grandfather, grandmother, father, mother, brother, or sister dies, for 7 days if the funeral is performed in this city, or for 7 days in addition to the period necessary for the trip to the native place where the funeral is performed.

At the end of every financial year, 10 per cent of the net profit for the year will be set aside as a fund for relief, consolation, and other co-operative purposes of the workers.

For regular workers there are similar rewards, a two weeks' trial period, and more regulations :

The work-day begins at 7 a.m. and ends at 5 p.m. The hours may be changed if necessary. There shall be the following rests every day : 15 minutes between 9 and 10 in the morning, 30 minutes at noon, and 15 minutes between 3 and 4 in the afternoon.

Holidays are as follows : The first and third Sunday every month, 5 days at New Year, 2 days in July, and 4 Great National Holidays : the New Year's Day on Jan. 1, the Anniversary of the Foundation of the Empire on Feb. 11, the Emperor's Birthday on April 29, and the Anniversary of the birth of the late Emperor Meiji on Nov. 3.

Workers are forbidden to play with fire or to smoke in the factory. They shall neither sing loudly nor gossip.

Wages will be calculated and paid on the 14th day of the month in the first half of the year, and on the last day of the month in the latter half of the year.

CHAPTER FIVE

WHY JAPAN SUCCEEDS

IS IT 'SOCIAL DUMPING'?

JAPAN'S civilization rests upon inexpensive foundations. The gay charm and beauty of Japanese social life do not, to any great extent, depend on wealth.

The chief materials of Japanese civilization are wood, bamboo, paper and straw, clay, coloured cloth, plants and flowers, all of which are relatively cheap.

The chief forms of Japanese civilization are ceremonial and patriarchal, non-individualistic. That applies to the style of work as well as to personal relationships. Thousands of years of tradition have caused these forms to be taken for granted.

The gifts of civilization being attainable, and its forms accepted by all but the very poorest, it follows that both are, in Japan, more widely spread among the masses than in any other country. What concerns us here is that a given unit of purchasing power represents probably more civilization in Japan than anywhere else in the world.

IN A WORKERS' STREET

In Japan the workers' districts in a large city, in a small town, or in an industrialized village, are very much alike. The low houses and the small shops are similar; space is limited within and without; electric light is one of the few modern amenities in general use. In the suburbs of large cities the rice-fields are as near the workers' homes as they are in the villages. Though statistics show that about three-fifths of the Japanese industrial population live in 'urban districts', they all dwell in small, large or vast village-like communities. Most of their houses are of wood. Stone and concrete buildings are not constructed in residential districts.

Gradually broad main roads are being built through the maze of narrow, though clean, streets. This has been necessary as a safety measure in case of fire, and because the traffic has increased. In these main roads are the larger shops, decorated with bright signs, flags and streamers, and brilliantly illuminated in many colours. Here also are the larger workshops, the cafés and restaurants, and often the schools, the cinemas and the small police stations. These main roads bring to the old-world residential districts some of the amenities of modern Western life.

The narrow streets, where road and pavement are one, where men and women can be seen praying at temples and shrines in secluded gardens, are lined with small, two-storied wooden dwellings. The sliding gratings, which serve as a window and a door, have thin wooden frames. Those opening out into the street are glazed, while white paper is pasted across those between the rooms. The houses, usually one-family dwellings, stand close together. At the back of some there are tiny gardens. These houses look attractive, though often neither healthy nor comfortable. Potted plants can be seen at many of the doors, but these, often ugly and stunted, reflect their owners' continuous struggle between poverty and a longing for beauty.

The Japanese workers live in these streets. Though they live the old traditional life, they have been influenced by modern achievements of the West. Probably nowhere in the West are bicycles or wireless sets more numerous. Nowhere do people read their newspapers more eagerly. And the numerous hairdressers, whose large American chairs seem out of place in these Oriental surroundings, are crowded from early morning until late at night. The women still wear kimonos, and the men wear cheap Western suits only for work, if at all. The temples and little shrines are as popular as are the inexpensive cinemas, featuring mainly historical Japanese films. During the day the women and children carry the babies tied to their backs ; this duty is taken over by the men when they come home from their work in the evening and have taken a hot bath in one of the many public baths. Perhaps the Japanese workers bow less deeply before their neighbours than they did, but their hands still glide ceremonially down to their knees, and they bow when they meet. The respect shown the male head of a family, especially by the women, has not abated. The men, who spend the day at their machines, are dignified and contented masters in their own homes in the evening.

The lower classes in Japan have little privacy. The sliding doors of their homes and workshops are rarely closed ; the shops are open, and people congregate in the streets. Within the family, consisting as most do of two generations, privacy is practically unknown. Whether the people like it or not, the family is merely a part of the larger community. People living in these districts are bound to each other by innumerable ties. One can see into the houses ; no curtains hide the view and many of the windows are unglazed. People can see each other at their meals, and, in the evening, when the older members of a family are still at work, one can see the children sleeping on the floor. On official cleaning days, which are supervised by the police, each family moves every movable object from the house into the road. Then the mats from the floors, the few pieces of furniture, clothes and bedding, household utensils, stores, tools—all are displayed to the public gaze.

THE WORKERS' SHOPS

In these narrow streets the shops are close together. There are rice shops with piles of straw-covered bundles, just as they arrive from the country. The rice flows in a glittering stream from modern polishing machines into tubs. Then there are tea shops, and shops which sell only spices. Others sell dried fish, or fish and fish cakes for special ceremonial use. There are shops for rice-wine and bean products—paste and curd and sauce and sweets, and for curious pastries and sweets, often made on the premises. These shops are frequently forced to compete with the street vendors for the children's mites. In the fruit and vegetable shops the goods, usually divided up into set quantities, are displayed on the floor or on low racks. In the meatshops small portions are offered for sale on paper plates; and cackling chicken are displayed in baskets or cages. There are shops selling charcoal, packed in bales of rice straw, and round little coal-cakes made of the waste of charcoal and pit-coal; others selling wooden footwear, material for kimonos, paper umbrellas, and others, again, selling bicycles, incandescent lamps, wireless sets, clocks and cheap jewellery.

The numerous stationery shops display high stacks of soft letter-size paper. The thin white qualities are carried in the kimono sleeve for use as a handkerchief, towel, or table napkin; the

1. Buying fish in front of the home

2. Retail shop for Japanese food—mainly dried fish and seaweed

coarse dark paper is used in the household. Even the poorest people choose the paper on which they write their letters with the greatest care.

In districts where many workers can barely afford the necessities of life, there are tobacco, chemist, book, and flower shops. Men and women who do not buy these luxuries for themselves purchase them at least to give away, for gifts are an important item in Japanese budgets.

The quality of the goods in these shops differs radically from that of the articles sold in the large stores, and fewer Western commodities are displayed. But here, too, the variety of the stock is surprising.

All shops are more or less specialized. Statistics show that there are 74 different kinds. In Tokyo alone there are almost 170,000 shops, an average of one for seven families. This does not include the innumerable workshops which give the workers' streets the appearance of a business rather than a residential district.

A DIFFERENT PROLETARIAT

The distinction between the workers, the artisans, and the small traders is less pronounced in Japan than it is in the West. These groups are really one, and a proletariat in the Western sense, where most families are entirely dependent upon industrial employment, exists only in a few centres. As a rule the situation is still ' semi-capitalistic ', and the workers' living conditions are quite different from those in the West.

Some members of a family may be employed in a factory, others occupied in agriculture or in home-work ; or they may own a small workshop or a miniature shop. When all the members of a family with a little money to spare are employed, they often go into partnerships with another family and open a small business. When the children are not working in the house, but their small earnings are needed, they are given work by neighbours who carry on home industries, or own a small workshop or shop.

Household work, too, is woven into this mosaic of activities. A woman who is a good seamstress but who is not employed in a factory or does not sew for the *geisha* houses, often sews for her neighbour. Some working women earn money by teaching others the art of Japanese flower arrangements, and some of the men cultivate dwarf trees, pines, maples and other plants not only for their own pleasure but on a business basis for their neighbours.

A man's hobby is sometimes almost as important as his regular occupation, which, as a rule, is not remunerative enough to support his family. The Japanese have a great capacity for work, and they are good business men. They like independence, and they are attracted by small capitalistic ventures in spite of increasing risks. The Japanese enjoy an occasional extravagance or speculation—both are national characteristics despite general thrift and modesty. Should a little capital be needed to start a new venture, it is not hard to come by. The Japanese save money even on very small incomes, and unlike other peoples they do it not so much for safety in emergencies, but in the hope of making some profitable investment. Forty million of the country's 65,000,000 inhabitants have post office saving accounts, and the average deposit amounts to 68 yen. About 20,000,000 of the population are insured at the Post Office for an average sum of about 130 yen. Another typically Japanese means of raising money is called *mujin*: the endless chain. Tens and hundreds of thousands of *mujin*, with an annual turnover of many hundreds of million yen, exist in Japan. It is probable that most families in the lower and the lower-middle classes belong to one of these *mujin*. Often they are large enterprises, under state supervision, but usually they are small private organizations including a group of friends or acquaintances. Here is an example: twenty individuals arrange to pay 10 yen a month into a co-operative account for two years. This means that the honorary cashier receives 200 yen a month. The *mujin* members meet once a month. A lottery is organized six times a year, and there is a single prize in the shape of a loan of 200 yen on which no interest is charged.

Moreover, six times a year an auction is organized. A loan is auctioned off which is to be redeemed at 200 yen, but the actual amount of which is determined by the bidding of the men present at the auction. The successful bid, that is the lowest, is sometimes very much below the nominal amount, and the difference represents the interest. A man can only participate in one such auction, and in the small *mujin* the sums left over at the end of the agreed period are distributed equally to all the members. The larger *mujin*, on the other hand, keep these remaining sums as a profit. Thus every one who has taken no risks at the auction gets back the money he invested in the *mujin*, and every loan is gradually liquidated by the monthly payments of the borrowing member.

By this and other methods many Japanese save a greater proportion of their current incomes, or spend or speculate more extravagantly than they can reasonably afford. They enjoy good food (meat when they can afford it) and they are very fond of *saké* (rice wine), but they willingly accept a mere subsistence standard of life in order to spend their savings on ceremonial acts, on investments or on certain luxuries. The traditional wage system, whereby large portions of the annual wages are paid in the form of bonuses, encourages this tendency. Bonuses are usually paid at New Year, and in the middle of the year at the time of the 'Feast of the Lanterns'. Wage-earners frequently spend their bonuses on luxurious entertainments or on splendid presents, unless they need the money for debts. Debts are important in Japan. The numerous pawnshops, as well as the prosperous usurers, whom it has been impossible to up-root, are symptomatic of the people's indebtedness.

'Capitalistic' enterprises, too, are stimulated by the prevailing system of wage payment. Unemployment insurance does not exist, and the dismissal fee, adjusted according to the period of past employment, enables many wage earners to become their own masters. It is typical of these conditions that the Tokyo Municipal Tramway Company, in 1934, ended a strike by reducing wages, and by formally dismissing the workers, so that their dismissal fees were paid. Then the men were re-employed. With their dismissal fees many tram conductors bought a share in a taxi or a small shop or workshop for a member of their family.

All these factors indicate how fundamentally the Japanese proletariat differs from the workers in other countries. They prevent the rise of 'class consciousness'—excepting perhaps among the ambitious lower-middle classes—and the life of Japanese wage earners is more interesting and satisfying, not despite, but because of, the risks involved in their mode of life.

The highly developed family system fundamentally differentiates the Japanese workers from the workers in the West. The family is responsible for social welfare, for old age pensions, for unemployment insurance, etc. And in Japan the family assumes these duties as a matter of course, just as the State does in the West. The family—including all branches and generations—thus becomes what the individual is in the West: the ultimate unit in the State. The head of a family, and men in general, enjoy privileges which compensate them for certain social disadvantages in their relationships outside the family. A worker in his own home is the equal of his employer at the factory.

A FAMILY OF EIGHT

A young working woman told us about her household. She was kneeling on the floor before the bowl of glowing charcoal. Her baby was tied to her back and she was rocking it gently. The woman was friendly but serious when she spoke. She had poise, and she was not shy.

There are eight in her family: her husband and herself; the baby and a little boy; her husband's older brother, his sister, his mother, and the wife's younger sister. This family is typical of old-fashioned Japanese family units, which are being gradually replaced by smaller families after the Western custom.

The man, a highly skilled transport worker, now earns—after a marked wage reduction—62 yen (£3 14*s.* 4*d.*) a month for a nine hours' working day. His sister, who is twenty-two,

Family kneeling by the low table for their meal—rice and fish
Note the infant on the mother's back

works eleven hours a day at a petrol station and earns 25 yen (£1 10s.). His wife's sister, who works eleven hours a day in a hosiery workshop, earns only half as much, 12.50 yen (15s.) a month. The man's mother is old, the brother is an invalid, and the young wife looks after the household. The income of this family, therefore, with three people at work, amounts to 99.50 yen (£6) a month.

Their rent is 21 yen (£1 5s.) a month. The house is draughty and small, but clean and attractive. There are two floors, with two rooms on each. Together the rooms are '17 mats' large. Each mat measures about two yards by one. The members of this family, like the workers in factory dormitories, each have about the space taken up by two mats, and every room is used as a bedroom at night. During the day the bedding is kept in cupboards, and only a few objects are kept on the spotless mats: a low table on which there is a bottle of ink and a writing brush, a small alarum clock and a few sewing tools. In the little heating bowl in the centre of the main room bits of charcoal glow continuously. A few kimonos hang on the bare walls. The small family shrine, Japanese landscape and some flowers, is in a corner of the room. A few cushions are on the floor. An electric light is suspended from the ceiling. This light, the alarum clock and a bicycle in the passage are the only modern objects in this house.

The woman got tea for us. She untied the baby and placed it gently on the floor, for outside in the kitchen it is cold and draughty, and cots or perambulators are not used in Japan. She then brought in her little household account book. Every day she inscribes neatly what she has spent. The items are written in Chinese characters, the prices in arabic figures. She also showed us the family wage envelopes, carefully tied together. Gradually we understood the family budget.

The quantity of rice needed by this family monthly—about 175 pounds at 11 sen a pound —costs about 19 yen (£1 2*s*. 9*d*.). Counting the two children as one person, each person consumes on an average about 13 ounces of rice a day. Another 10 sen (1½*d*.) a day is spent for other food: for the cheap but nourishing bean paste (*miso*) costing 1¼*d*. a pound, from which the breakfast soup is prepared by the addition of a little rice and tea or hot water; for vegetables (costing from ½*d*. to 1½*d*. a pound) and ingredients needed for the rice dinner; for a little meat (2*d*. to 4*d*. a pound), pickles or sweetened potatoes, or bean curd (*tofu*) taken with the rice for the evening meal. A small proportion of this 10 sen a day is spent on 'odds and ends'.

The woman spends 3 or 4 yen a month (3*s*. 7*d*. to 4*s*. 9*d*.) for the scanty heating arrangements (the room is never really warm in the winter); for electric light and the regular hot bath in the public baths, which usually costs 1 or 2 sen a person. A newspaper costs 1 yen (1*s.* 2*d.*) a month, the monthly magazine costs ½ yen (7*d.*) and occasionally a member of the family spends 10 sen (½*d.*) at the cinema.

The clothing of the entire family of eight costs only 80 to 100 yen a year (£4 16*s.* to £6) but the housewife does not include these sums in her monthly budget, for they are paid from the annual bonus, which is about equal to a month's wages.

'We are poor because we are a large family,' the woman said, 'and we are not really contented, but the main point is that the children have everything they need.'

The expenses of this family, however, only absorb about two-thirds of the income: about 67 yen are spent (not counting clothing), which means that about 30 yen are left over. 'This sum is not included in the household budget,' the woman told us. The family pays 12 yen a month on old debts and 20 yen into the *mujin*. The man got into debt when, in the hope of increasing the family income, he bought a share in a taxi for his brother. The partnership failed, however, the taxi was sold at auction and the debts remained.

A WELL-TO-DO FAMILY

A young foreman in the bicycle factory described earlier in this book told us about his family budget. We were in the little reception-room of the works and the red, gold-embroidered factory flag hung underneath the shrine in the corner of the room. The man is twenty-eight. He has been employed in the factory for fifteen years and is now in charge of a department. He earns 59 yen (£5 18*s*. at par; £3 11*s*. at present rates) a month. His normal working day begins at seven o'clock in the morning. He has an hour's rest at noon and two free days a month, and he works until five o'clock in the afternoon. He also earns 15 yen a month for three and a half hours overtime on twenty-six days (from five-thirty in the afternoon to nine o'clock in the evening). As a member of the works council he receives another 5 yen a month from the management. His total monthly income is therefore 79 yen (£7 18*s*. at par; £4 15*s*. at present rates). That is considerably above the average earnings in Japan. The 100 yen which he receives annually as a bonus do not affect the monthly budget, for he told us that he spends most of this sum on presents and on New Year's celebrations.

This man supports only his wife and their baby. Before the infant's birth the wife earned 25 yen a month by sewing lovely kimonos for the *geisha* houses.

The rent of the new little house, which he showed us proudly, is 13 yen (£1 6*s*. at par; 15*s*. 6*d*. at present rates) a month. Coal, gas, electric light and water cost about half this sum.

They spend a little less than 1 yen (2*s.* at par; 1*s.* 6*d.* at present rates) daily for food. A third of this sum is spent on rice; a tenth for milk; and the rest for vegetables, bean products, spices, fish, and for meat once a week.

Average monthly expenditure for clothing amounts to not more than 3 yen (6*s.* at par; 3*s.* 6*d.* at present rates) for the whole family. The man's compulsory and the woman's voluntary health insurance costs about the same amount. Half of his insurance is paid by the factory. He spends another 3 yen for his newspaper, a magazine and the cinema. On his two free days he allows himself the luxury of fishing with two friends. This costs him 2 yen.

He saves 15 or 20 yen a month—about what he earns for overtime—and he deposits this sum regularly in his post office savings account. He is contented, and he is justified in thinking himself fortunate.

A HARD-WORKING FAMILY

A mechanic at the pencil 'combine' described in an earlier chapter told us about his complicated family budget. He was taking tea with his employer in the little office-reception-room where accounts and samples are kept.

This man has two sources of income. As a mechanic he earns 33 yen a month. He works every day from seven o'clock in the morning to six o'clock in the evening, with an hour's rest at noon and two free days a month. While the export trade is as prosperous as it is at present, he receives a month's wages as a bonus every six months.

He earns a second income as a small employer. He and his wife work at home for the pencil factory, and they employ three neighbours' children to help them. When he comes home from the factory he rests for a short time, and after his wife has seen to her two little children and the household, she and her husband work three hours in the evening. They also devote most of the two free days a month to this home-work. After the children's wages have been paid, this man has 14 yen a month from this second source of income, his total earnings being 47 yen (£4 15*s.* at par; £2 16*s.* 5*d.* at present rates), excluding bonuses.

His house, near the factory, is small and old. It has room for 10 mats, and the rent is only 9 yen a month. He spends about 3 yen a month on coal, gas and electric light. He pays 0.60 yen a month for his health insurance; the factory pays the other half. His wife and children are not insured.

This family's average daily expenditure for food is 0.60 yen (1*s.* 2½*d.* at par; 8½*d.* at the present rate of exchange). They spend about 4 yen a month on clothing (8*s.* at par; 4*s.* 10*d.* at the present rate of exchange); and about 5 yen for *saké*, tobacco and the cinema. The man saves about 6 yen a month.

JAPANESE DIET

It is clear from earlier statements that a Japanese family spends less on food than its counterpart in the West. There are two reasons for this: the average quantity of foodstuffs consumed by the Japanese is smaller, and the average quality of food per unit of weight consumed is inferior. The apparent cheapness of Japanese foodstuffs, on the other hand, is often deceptive.

Let us first consider the smaller amount consumed. According to *The Food of Japan*, published by the League of Nations in 1933, the average daily amount of food consumed per head of the population is less than 3 pounds. This figure is, of course, based on an equal distribution of the national food supplies (96 per cent of which are domestic products) to the entire population. Three pounds is not much more than an English unemployed man requires to ‘ permit working capacity to be maintained ’, as is stated in the British Medical Association's famous ‘ Report of the Committee on Nutrition ’, published in 1933. The actual daily food consumption of the English population is, of course, much higher than the diet ‘ prescribed ’ by the B.M.A. for the unemployed.

The wealthier classes in Japan naturally consume more than three pounds of food per day per head, and this three pounds average might therefore imply that other groups of the population are living on a starvation level. And as the sections of the nation who live above that average, if not as numerous as in Western countries, are still very large, it would appear that under-nourishment is very general in Japan. This is not the case, however, for actually Japan's food supplies are not quite as small as they seem. The weight of normal, healthy Japanese—men, women and children—is about a fifth less than the weight of corresponding persons in the West, and their height is substantially smaller. The relative physiological food requirements depend upon the size and the weight of the body. This means that, from the employer's point of view, the Japanese worker, who needs less food, is cheaper than the Western wage earner, provided that productivity is the same.

A comparison between the Japanese and the English quality per weight unit of food is less favourable to Japan. The best comparable figures are probably the average diet per head per day available in Japan and the diet 'prescribed' by the B.M.A. for an English family, consisting of an unemployed man, his wife and his child of eight. The Japanese figures represent roughly a maximum living standard, while the English figures are minimum standards. The former may be above, while the other is below, the real consumption. The comparison of the two standards, therefore, actually understates the difference between them.

1. Bleaching towel cloth in the air. One of the typical scenes in Osaka
2. Women transplanting rice in the paddy field

Per Head per Day.	Japanese Diet (Average National Supply).	English Diet (Unemployed Family).
	oz.	oz.
Cereals	21.0	18.3
Dry legumes . . .	2.3	1.1
Potatoes, vegetables, fruit .	18.5	10.0
Meat, fish, fat, dairy products	3.8	12.8
Sugar	1.2	4.2
	46.8 oz.	46.4 oz.
Average price per lb. of food.	. 9.3 sen [1]	$2\frac{3}{4}d.$

The Japanese diet lacks animal albumen, fats and sugar. The quality of Japanese food is also affected by the relative shortage of protein and vitamins in rice, Japan's most important foodstuff, as compared with bread, the staple food of Western peoples. Most pickled Japanese vegetables and roots, furthermore, do not contain important vitamins, which further affects the quality of Japanese food. The League of Nations reports as follows about this subject :

> The consumption of quantity without quality is in some respects more dangerous than starvation, for the latter is obvious and a remedy is sought ; the former may remain a hidden source of evil. This appears to be the great danger in Japan.

Most Japanese have always lived on such a diet ; yet the population has increased, and developed a great capacity for work. The Japanese death rate is the lowest in the East, though it is larger by half than the English death rate. Since the Nineteenth Century the *per capita* consumption of cereals in Japan has

[1] $2\frac{1}{4}d.$ at par ; $1\frac{1}{3}d.$ at present exchange rate.

increased by about 20 per cent and that of fish has trebled, but the problem of the quantitative, and above all the qualitative, food supply is still very serious.

Believers in the theory of Japan's '*social dumping*' attribute this situation to the low wage level. Actually, however, this food problem has resulted from Japan's poverty in agricultural resources. The only peaceful solution would be an increase in Japan's exports of manufactures. In return, she could import from abroad raw materials as well as the foodstuffs necessary to raising the standard of living. Only then would a rise in wages be really useful.

THE AGRARIAN BACKGROUND

Prices for essential foodstuffs are not lower in Japan than in other countries. The comparisons shown above indicate that since the depreciation of the yen the price per pound of important foodstuffs in Japan are about half of English prices for staple foodstuffs. At par, however, staple Japanese foodstuffs, though of far lower quality, are only about 18 per cent cheaper than English foodstuffs.

If, however, comparable groups of foods in Japan and in England are considered, it is apparent that Japanese domestic prices are about 20 per cent higher, at par, than English prices. If prices are compared at their par value, even the retail price of rice is about 16 per cent higher in Japan than in London. Besides, the retail profit is smaller in Japan than in England. To-day the price of rice in Japan seems lower only because of the yen depreciation. Wheat-flour, an increasingly important foodstuff in Japan, costs 2*d.* a pound at par in Tokyo; in London the price is only a little above 1*d.*

Despite these relatively high prices Japanese farmers are anything but prosperous. They try to make both ends meet by breeding silkworms, by home industries or by continual personal sacrifices. How can this paradox be explained?

The extraordinary natural poverty of the country provides the explanation. A shortage of good land and the growing population has forced farmers to cultivate 'marginal' land and to increase their crops, even though their labours are unprofitable if regarded in terms of money.

As Japan becomes more modern, her public expenditures increase. Agriculture represents the largest group of the population, and as the farmers are least able to offer resistance, they are burdened with tremendous direct and indirect taxes, which, in turn, increase production costs and decrease net earnings. Apart from taxation, the farmers pay high rents, and high rates of interest on their ever-growing debts. The Imperial Agricultural Society reports that in 1933 taxation and interest rates included in the total production costs of rice were 50 per cent higher than the labour costs involved.

A reduction of costs by means of rationalization is impossible because of the abundance of agricultural labour and lack of capital. The low purchasing power in urban districts furthermore has prevented a permanent rise in prices of agricultural products.

Japanese agriculture, against the heaviest odds, produces almost the entire food supply for an increasing population. It is no longer as simple as it was to provide cheap food for industrial workers. In England it is done by importing foodstuffs from overseas. In Japan this is impossible, and Japanese agriculture is now artificially depressed in order that Japanese industrial workers (and thus the Japanese export trade) can compete successfully in foreign markets. For if agricultural prices were high enough to give the Japanese farmer a decent living standard, it would be impossible for Japanese industry to compete successfully. Even now food prices in Japan are relatively high, and the Japanese worker counteracts them by a modest quantity consumption and a still more modest quality demand. The Bureau of Statistics of the Imperial Cabinet estimates that the monthly *per capita* expenditure for food of well-paid industrial workers averages only 8.75 yen (17*s*. 6*d*. at par; 10*s*. 6*d*. at the present rate of exchange) and of salaried workers 10.06 yen (£1 or 12*s*.).

HOUSING AND CLOTHING

Building costs are lower in Japan than in the West, because Japanese houses are so much simpler. A worker's dwelling with two or three rooms costs only about 1,200 yen (£120 at par; £72 at the present rate of exchange). Often the site alone is responsible for three-quarters of this sum. Despite these low building costs, rents are relatively high and represent as much as 20 per cent of the worker's budget. This is due to high rates of interest and the high profits made by the landlords. A semi-public building company in Tokyo, which gave us these figures, mentioned that in many cases the landlords recover their building costs in seven or eight years, or even sooner; and Japanese wooden houses last a very long time.

In a typical Tokyo district investigated by this company, 86 per cent of the families rent the houses in which they live: only 6 per cent of the residents own their homes, while the rest rent single rooms or live in company dwellings. Of these workers' families 18 per cent live in one to three rooms, though in 65 per cent of them there are more than four persons in the family.

Nineteen per cent of these families pay less than 10 yen a month rent (£1 at par; 12*s*. at the present rate of exchange); 42 per cent pay between 10 and 15 yen; 28 per cent pay between 15 and 20 yen. The Bureau of Statistics of the Imperial Cabinet estimates that the average housing costs *per capita* per month in well-paid workers' families amount to 4.12 yen (8*s*. 2*d*. at par; 4*s*. 9*d*. at the present rate of exchange). High as these rents are for the Japanese worker, they are below rents in the West, and represent a wage advantage to Japanese industry.

Differences in housing conditions of the workers and the middle classes in Japan are less noticeable than they are in the West. Both groups benefit by the mild season in Japan, which lasts about three-quarters of the year and makes thin-walled houses possible. Both working and middle-class families, on the other hand, suffer cold and draught in the winter, for the rooms are practically unheatable. Both classes profit from the aesthetic tradition which demands that rooms are left almost bare; both have satisfactory sanitary arrangements, though they have not yet attained Western standards.

Though the housing conditions of Japanese workers are bad, they cannot be called a form of 'social dumping', at least not as long as so many Western wage-earners live in slums. Western slums are no better than those in Japan, and the average dwellings in Japan are quite as satisfactory as comparable homes in the West.

As we have seen, Japanese workers spend very little on clothing. Wooden shoes, cotton clothes and underclothes are the chief items. A minimum amount of clothing is needed during the long summer, when a woollen cummerbund is the only garment worn, not only for reasons of decency, but for hygienic reasons as well. In the winter, for which, in this as in other directions, the Japanese style of living is not really suited, the poor people's clothing is not warm enough.

The Bureau of Statistics of the Imperial Cabinet estimates the *per capita* expenditure for clothing a month among workers' families at 2.07 yen (4*s*. at par; and 2*s*. 5*d*. at the present rate of exchange), and in the families of salaried men at 3.05 (6*s*. or 3*s*. 7*d*.).

Even when a saving on prime necessities is involved Japanese families put aside something for cultural outlays (health, amusement, education, social). The family budgets investigated in this connexion by the Bureau of Statistics are based on earnings which are a little above the average. In workers' families these cultural expenditures *per capita* per month amount to 3.82 yen (7*s*. 7*d*. at par; 4*s*. 7*d*. at the present rate of exchange); in families of salaried men to 5.98 (12*s*.; or 7*s*. 2*d*.). These sums may seem small, but as we have seen, prices for these items are low. It is probable, furthermore, that families which spend these sums for cultural purposes derive a greater satisfaction from them —typically Japanese satisfaction based on traditions—than most workers' families in the West could derive even at a little higher outlay. This section of the family budget illustrates the advantages of a high, though cheaply run, civilization.

THE TREND OF REAL WAGES

After this brief sketch of Japan's social conditions it is necessary to consider the probable trend of their development, which will influence Japan's competitive exports considerably.

Undoubtedly the living standards of industrial workers are higher than they were in the nineteenth century. Undoubtedly, also, the agricultural population has not experienced the same improvement.

But what has been the trend of real wages in industry during the last few years? The year 1926, when the effects of the earthquake and the fire of 1923 were no longer felt, will serve as a basis for wages developments. In 1926 the real wages, that is to say the purchasing power of wages, were 55 per cent higher than in 1914. From 1926 to 1931 nominal wages dropped by about 20 per cent. Retail prices, however, fell by about one-third as a result of the agricultural depression, the rise in unemployment, and the international collapse of prices. The purchasing power of industrial wages, therefore, was actually 82 per cent higher than in 1914, chiefly at the cost of the farmers. It should be mentioned, however, that the retail price index on which these figures are based does not include rents, which apparently remained more stable than the costs for clothing or food, and for this reason the ultimate result may be rather less favourable for the industrial workers.

Since 1931 nominal wages have, with some fluctuations, decreased by about 8 per cent, but retail prices have risen (by about 15 per cent from 1931 to the end of 1934). This rise is due largely to the yen depreciation.

Real wages, therefore, were not much higher at the end of 1934 than in 1926, but they were 60 per cent above the 1914 level. The continuity of this rise stopped at a time when Japanese industry was particularly prosperous, and there are many reasons for believing that the interruption of this upward trend may be of more than temporary importance.

This matter will be discussed later, but it should be emphasized here that a country which can increase real wages by 60 per cent in the space of two decades is in a position to decrease them again, if necessary. Difficulties in keeping foreign export markets might cause such a decline. Meanwhile, as long as this rate of progress is maintained, it cannot be stated that Japan is applying the method known as 'social dumping'.

CHAPTER SIX

IS IT THE YEN?

THE SIGNAL FROM LONDON

ON the twenty-first of September 1931 a part of the Japanese export trade suddenly came to a standstill. Great Britain had gone off the gold standard, the pound fell, and the yen, dependent on gold, rose in relation to sterling.

Japanese export goods, valued at 1,000 yen, which had cost £100 the day before on British markets—for at par 1 yen is about 2*s*.—suddenly cost £130. The price of British competitive goods, on the other hand, did not change. By December of that year the price for the same Japanese goods was as high as £150 sterling.

Similar developments occurred on other markets: British goods were at first cheaper by a fourth and later by a third—in dollars, guldens, francs, pesos, yen. Export prices for Japanese goods, however, continued unchanged.

The equilibrium on competitive world markets was disturbed. The weakest countries were most severely hit. The depreciation of the pound sounded the alarm.

BREAKING THE CHAINS OF GOLD

At this time Japan was dissatisfied with the gold standard, which had been introduced early in 1930 after a painful period of deflation. 'Retrenchment' was the Government's slogan. 'Liberal spending, if need be by means of inflation', was the answer of those who were governed.

The masses of the population employed in the semi-feudal branches of industry and trade—the peasants, artisans, small industrialists, and traders—suffered as a result of the low prices paid for their products; competition was severe and credit conditions were bad. The crisis grew worse, and agriculture was particularly affected. Deflation had brought nothing but disadvantages to these sections of the population, and the gold standard threatened to perpetuate their difficulties.

The deflation policy, directed first at the reintroduction and then at the maintenance of the gold standard, had been a disadvantage to military and naval interests as well. For, as a result of this policy, the expenditure on armaments had been decreased. Also agriculture, the army's 'first line of defence', the source of fresh recruits, had been weakened, while industry and finance, suspected of internationalism, were strengthened. Military and political men in Japan began to take an interest in economic matters, and to participate, gropingly at first and then more firmly, in the development of present and future economic policies.

The differences between the 'old' and the 'new' Japan increased the discontent in the country. The 'new' capitalist Japan, co-operating with political parties, seemed responsible for the industrial policies which had been adopted. Corruption, either real or imaginary, intensified the popular hatred of the deflationary policy. The radical patriots, who are not unlike the National Socialists in Germany, were particularly enraged, and they finally killed the Finance Minister, Inouye, who was responsible for the deflation, and Baron Dan, one of the leading financiers of the country. The Premier, Inuka, too, was murdered by patriots, for, though he broke the chains of gold, he did not encourage 'liberal spending', despite the distress of farmers and small traders.

The modern section of Japanese industry at first actually benefited by the deflation. The banks, amalgamated and strengthened, had been put back on a sound basis. Large industries liquidated their debts and were modernized and rationalized. Lesser industries followed suit, especially those attached to the great combines. Industry was organized on a larger and more promising scale than ever before.

On the other hand, industry and finance had been adversely affected by the wholesale dismissals of workers and the drop in wages, accompanying the process of rationalization, by the general results of the deflation, and by the world economic crisis. Domestic purchasing power and the demand of foreign markets decreased markedly, and both were hopelessly small in relation to the growing capacity of Japan's modernized industry. In the long run, the deflation and the gold standard, having done their duty, could only bring harm to industry.

The Army was the first to break through the chains of gold—probably unconsciously—when on the eighteenth of September 1931, three days before England left the gold standard, it began to occupy Manchuria. This operation involved Japan in political and financial consequences which could not be reconciled with deflation, with retrenchment, or with the maintenance of the gold standard. The abandonment of the gold standard, the fall of the yen, ' liberal spending ' by the Government, perhaps an inflation, all these developments were now only a question of time.

Such was Japan's position when England announced that she had abandoned the gold standard. As it now seemed impossible to prevent a fall of the yen without tremendous sacrifices, many industrialists and financiers speculated in exchanges and raw materials, thus hastening the fall of the currency. In a few weeks the Bank of Japan lost almost half its gold holdings. A Cabinet crisis occurred, and the first decision of the new Government, announced on December 13th, 1931, one day after it came into power, was that the country would go off the gold standard.

On September 18th, 1931, the 'Manchurian Incident' marked the beginning of a new period in Japan's political expansion. On December 13th, when Japan left the gold standard, she began a new period of economic expansion on world markets. From that day dates, if not the actual start of the great Japanese export drive, at least the creation of its most important impetus.

THE FALL OF THE YEN

The yen began to fall. At first it followed the pound. In January 1932 the two currencies had regained parity. A yen, which had temporarily been worth 3*s*., was again worth 2*s*.

Once more Japanese export goods worth 1,000 yen cost £100 on British markets. Japan had recaptured her former price relation to British goods on world markets, but the hoped-for increase of sales did not occur. The world depression was in full swing, and most of the would-be buyers in foreign countries were waiting to see whether the yen would not depreciate further.

The yen continued to fall, while sterling remained practically stable. At the end of 1932 the yen was not worth much more than 1*s*. 3*d*., and soon it sank to about 1*s*. 2*d*., where it remained during 1933 and 1934.

Many Japanese export goods valued at 1,000 yen which had cost £100 at par, were suddenly worth a little less than £60 on British markets. Their gold price had dropped from $500 to $175. Gradually exports began to revive and the boom started.

In relation to sterling the yen had fallen by more than 40 per cent, in relation to gold by about 60 per cent.

To what extent can this 40 or 60 per cent currency advantage really be exploited by Japanese exporters against their foreign competitors?

To what extent does the depreciation of the yen stimulate exports, or, in other words, constitute an 'export premium' or bounty?

The theoretical answer to this question would be: to the extent to which the domestic purchasing power of the yen remains higher than its foreign, depreciated value.

The practical answer, however, cannot be formulated briefly or in exact figures. Let us try to find the practical answer by determining the influence of the depreciation of the yen on the various costing factors contributing to the total price of Japanese export goods.

THE EXTENT OF THE EXPORT PREMIUM

Obviously, Japan must now pay more for foreign raw materials in depreciated yen than she paid in gold yen. And, as has been pointed out, two-thirds of the raw materials contained in Japanese export goods are purchased abroad.

For this reason it is often assumed that Japanese exporters of, say, cotton, wool or rubber goods, are losing some of the financial advantage they would otherwise derive from the depreciated currency. This is not the case. For when a raw material needed for the manufacture of an exported article is a world-market commodity—such as cotton, wool or rubber—the competition between the exporters of the finished product is normally confined to the *margin* between the price of the finished product and the price of the raw materials used in its manufacture.

All manufacturers of cotton, wool or rubber goods must, of course, pay the same price—that is to say the world-market price—for the same raw material, regardless of the currency in their own country or in the country in which the raw material is purchased.

These manufacturers must include in the total price quoted to their customers the same price for the raw material used, no matter in what currency their goods are offered for sale.

The higher yen-costs for world-market raw materials are therefore not a negative but a neutral factor in Japanese export competition. They do not affect the essential factor in international competition—the margin between the price of raw materials and the finished product.

Such world-market raw materials as raw silk or copper, which are produced in Japan, are also a neutral factor in the international competition as far as Japanese exporters of finished products are concerned. For raw silk, which is now so cheap, can be bought in Japan at the same price by British or American manufacturers of silk goods as by their Japanese competitors. And Japanese copper normally follows world-market prices by increasing the prices quoted in depreciated yen.

The freight charges for world-market raw materials, however, are the first item entering into the margin for which there is international competition. In so far as Japanese ships are used to import raw materials the depreciation of the yen is an advantage to Japanese manufacturers. For the large Japanese merchant fleet, subsidized by the State, virtually extends the territory of domestic transport, where the yen has practically retained its value, to the whole world. On the whole, the depreciated yen can to-day buy more shipping space than the current equivalent in sterling or gold. This is true not only of imports of raw materials but of exports of finished products as well. As far as freight charges are concerned, therefore, the depreciation of the yen works almost fully as an export premium.

A second item entering into the margin for which there is international competition, are such raw materials and materials needed in the manufacture of export goods which, for various reasons, are not as much subject to international price arbitrage as are, for instance, cotton, rubber, copper, &c. In other words, these raw materials are not world-market products but the products of sheltered national industries: they include raw materials used in the manufacture of potteries, various chemicals, building materials, coal, iron, &c. Indirectly, however, the prices for these materials are somewhat influenced by world markets, and for various domestic reasons these prices have increased in Japan by an average of 30 per cent since the depreciation of the yen. This means that actually the depreciated yen purchases a little less of these materials than can be bought for the equivalent in sterling or gold. For these products of sheltered national industries the depreciation of the yen, at the end of 1934, constituted an export premium only to the extent of about 50 per cent.

The third and most important item entering into the margin for which there is international competition, an item which is often more than 50 per cent and sometimes not much less than 100 per cent of that margin, are the wage costs. Wages have not been affected by the outward depreciation of the yen, or better said: the wage decreases outweighed the wage increases, which occurred chiefly in the metal and armament trades. Since the abandonment of the gold standard, that is to say from the end of 1931 to the end of 1934, wages decreased on an average by 8 per cent, despite the fact that living costs in Japan during the same period increased by about 15 per cent. The yen of the Japanese worker has been depreciated, but the wage-yen of the Japanese manufacturer buys slightly more labour to-day than it did in 1931.

As far as wages are concerned, therefore, the depreciation of the yen is fully exploited as an export premium.

The fourth and last item entering into the margin for which there is international competition are the machinery, overhead and capital costs of production. On the whole, the costs for new machinery have risen. Even for foreign machinery, however, these costs have hardly kept pace with the fall of the yen, because the Japanese market for foreign machinery is shrinking and competition has frequently forced down prices in sterling or gold. Rents, salaries, and taxes have remained unchanged, and in 1935 only the excess profits tax is to be increased. Higher yen payments on foreign debts are important only in isolated cases, and money rates in Japan have decreased. In this section, too, the purchasing power of the yen is about as great as it was before the depreciation.

The depreciation of the yen constitutes a premium on exports in the following degrees:

wage costs:
  to the full extent of the depreciation
machinery, overhead, &c., costs:
  almost to the full extent
cost for domestic materials:
  to about half the extent

freight costs :
almost to the full extent.

It is obvious, therefore, that, whatever the costing factors of Japanese export goods, the Japanese exporter enjoys a great exchange advantage over his foreign competitor.

WHO PAYS FOR THE PREMIUM ON EXPORTS?

To a certain extent this export premium pays for itself by increasing the turnover and the profits of Japanese export industries and by stimulating trade throughout the country. To an even larger extent, however, other economic groups have to pay the cost of the advantages gained by the exporters.

The rise in yen prices of foreign raw materials is a neutral factor for the export industries ; for Japanese consumers, however, who need finished articles manufactured largely from foreign raw materials this rise is a great burden, especially as their incomes are unchanged unless for the worse.

Furthermore, the Japanese export trade is not concerned with rising costs of living, for so far they have not affected wages. And even the rise in prices of certain domestic materials means only a small decrease in the export premium. Domestic consumers, however, are seriously affected by both rises.

Japan has suffered more from the depreciation of

the yen than Great Britain has from the fall of the pound, not only because the fall of the yen has been greater, but also for two other reasons:

In England the depreciation of the currency is compensated for not only, as in Japan, by an increase in exports, but by the protection it affords to domestic British markets against foreign competition, for the depreciation of the pound has had the same effect as a raising of the tariff. In Japan the disadvantages connected with the depreciation of the yen were not counteracted in this way, because her inland markets were already protected by high customs duties and by ingrained habits of consumption.

Though English consumers paid higher sterling prices for foreign raw materials after the currency depreciation, the overhead charges for domestic consumption goods, and sometimes their sale prices, decreased as production for export increased. In Japan, on the other hand, such an adjustment did not occur to the same extent, because industrial concerns manufacturing for domestic and foreign trade, are less often identical than they are elsewhere.

As these developments indicate, Japan did not depreciate her currency easily or with the intention of stimulating her export trade, any more than England did. These facts also prove that the currency depreciation has not been of sufficient advantage to Japanese industry and trade as a whole for the experiment to be repeated merely to increase the export trade.

For actually the yen-depreciation became only effective as an export premium because real wages were decreased. Should a further lowering of real wages prove necessary, it could probably be attained more easily and more cheaply by a change in domestic policy than by a further decline of the yen which, apart from all other evils, would increase the artificial barriers against Japanese exports.

THE FUTURE OF THE YEN

Is it probable that imperative reasons will again cause a fall of the yen, and that the Japanese export premium will thus be increased?

To answer this question, the foreign and domestic financial situation of the country must be considered.

Japan's international balance of payments, which reflects the state of her foreign finances, was always precarious. War contributions, foreign loans raised after military victories, and lastly, enormous profits during the World War, were the extraordinary means by which her recurring difficulties were overcome and unfavourable fluctuations of the yen avoided. The considerable loss of gold which the Bank of Japan suffered towards the end of 1931 immediately before the fall of the yen, meant that Japan had exhausted the financial windfall acquired during the World War.

Contrary to her former victories, the 'Manchurian incident ' brought in its train no financial benefits. On the contrary, it has so far proved a burden. Nor does the present export boom mean a new financial windfall, for Japan has had particularly large payments abroad to meet during recent years for stock reserves of certain raw materials. Even rising exports could never quite keep pace with imports bought in pursuance of her military policy for ' emergencies '.

Nevertheless, Japan has succeeded in adjusting her balance of payments without credits from abroad. And her foreign debts are not much greater than her assets in foreign countries, though these are chiefly ' frozen ' in Manchuria and China.

Unless unforeseen losses occur, Japan's foreign finances should not necessitate a further depreciation of the yen in the immediate future. The margin of safety, however, is small, and a sudden decrease in exports might result in a weakening of the yen, if, at the same time, for military and political reasons, imports of raw materials were increased beyond the normal domestic and manufacturing demands.

When Japan came off the gold standard in 1931, external circumstances supplied merely the last impetus, while internal causes were chiefly responsible for the depreciation. In the same way the future movement of the yen will depend largely upon the financial policy of Japan's rulers.

The estimates for the Army and Navy in the

Budget 1935–6 amounted to nearly 50 per cent of the record Budget of over 2,000,000,000 yen; this is exactly twice as much as the Services used in the average of 1922–32. They actually received one-fifth more than the total revenue of the State from taxes and import duties.

The expenditure of Army and Navy strongly influences Japan's international balance of payments. On the amount of the Army and Navy estimates depends the measure of raw material imports for armament purposes. At present these purchases seem to be mainly responsible for the large excess of imports over exports. The amount available for Manchukuo also depends on the size of the estimates of the fighting Services. In the interests of the stability of the yen Mr. Takahashi, the Finance Minister, early in 1935 protested against the large sums ear-marked for Manchukuo. At the same time, however, Mr. Hayashi, the Minister for War, stated in the Diet that 'it would be impossible to guarantee that the sum allotted would be sufficient for the needs of the Army'.

INFLATION?

Japan's Government finances, too, have always depended upon occasional windfalls. The boom during the World War was the last windfall of this kind. The reserves left over from these fortunate times, reserves which took the form of a surplus from old Budgets, helped to balance the new Budgets until shortly before the currency devaluation. When these reserves were exhausted, retrenchment became doubly necessary.

After Japan abandoned the gold standard, Government expenditure rose rapidly. For the necessity, or the wish, to increase that expenditure had been one of the chief motives for leaving gold. As ordinary State revenue, on the other hand, did not increase but declined somewhat, Budget deficits rose sharply. From this time onwards, an annual average of a third of the total Government expenditures had to be financed by the issue of public loans. The greater part of the income from these loans was spent on armaments and on interest on former loans; a small proportion of this income was spent on agricultural relief, which was never sufficient.

From the end of 1931 to the end of 1934 the internal debt of the State was thus doubled to almost 9,000,000,000 yen. It will probably continue to increase during the next few years, for any considerable curtailment of Government expenditure, or substantial increase in revenues, are not probable.

Despite these inflationary policies, there are no symptoms in Japan which would indicate that a real inflation exists. The circulation of notes has not increased to any marked extent. On the contrary, in relation to the average activity of trade and to the yen value of the total turnover it has decreased and is now lower than it was before the depreciation of the yen. It is more correct, therefore, to speak of the financial situation in Japan as a continuing deflation.

This paradoxical situation is easy to explain: Japan's economic life is virtually divided into two camps, which develop independently of each other. The larger, semi-feudal section, comprising agriculture and sericulture, small and medium-sized industries and the retail trade are suffering an acute depression. These branches of trade and manufacture are now hardly able to obtain credit; they are hit by low prices and heavy debts; in short, they pay interest to the modernized section of trade and industry, which is generally prosperous. In this modern camp more or less large profits are being made by the armament plants, by the export industries, by the banks and financial concerns. Though as great a proportion of these profits as possible is re-invested, considerable 'liquid' capital remains in the banks, which are also accumulating the interest payments of the semi-feudal section. For all this surplus capital almost the only safe and paying investment at present are Government bonds, which still pay a relatively high rate of interest. These bonds are therefore a blessing for large financial interests.

The second cause for the deflationist results of Japan's inflation policy is the successful prevention of a general rise in wages and salaries, and, as far as possible, of prices. The former is made possible without artificial means by the oversupply of labour; the latter by the chronic depression of agriculture. Thus the inflation does not exist except in the records of the banks and it stops before it reaches the consumer or the printing presses. The internal value of the yen not being lowered by wage or price increases, a real inflation has been avoided—at least for the time being.

The day of reckoning must come, however, for the thousands of millions spent by the Government on armaments and other expenditures will have to be met eventually.

Perhaps this day of reckoning will be as pleasant as Japan dreams that it may be; when world prosperity has replaced world depression; when exports of finished products, as well as of raw silk, increase in price and in quantity; when the domestic demand has risen; when investments in Manchuria have proved profitable; when, in fact, conditions have so improved that, with or without an increase in taxation, Japan will be in a position to pay her accumulated debts from a well-balanced Budget.

But the day of reckoning may be very stormy: these hopes may not be fulfilled. The capital market may no longer be able to absorb large loans; industrialists may be frightened, or need the capital, and withdraw their money from the banks; it may be necessary to use the printing presses; prices and wages may no longer be held back. Then the 'beneficent' inflation may turn quickly into a 'malignant' inflation, as some sceptics already fear it may. It may even get so far out of control as to cause a further depreciation of the yen which might no longer be an advantage.

CHAPTER SEVEN

POLITICS AND ECONOMICS

IS IT STATE ASSISTANCE?

THREE successive wars brought Japanese industry into existence; two successive national emergencies sharply accelerated its development. For five decades, in an almost mathematical rhythm of ten-year periods, one extraordinary stimulus to industry followed another:

The Chinese War of 1894–5, which made the first industrial demands on the country, began this development. After centuries of trance in economic feudalism Japan had just laid the foundations of a modern industrial life. The victorious war gave her new territory, war indemnities, a new spirit of enterprise, prestige and foreign credits.

The war with Russia in 1904–5 made still greater industrial demands on Japan, but she was now better prepared to meet them. The victory over a Great Power brought new territory and enhanced influence, increased both her self-confidence and her foreign credits, and caused another industrial expansion.

The World War of 1914–18 laid open the world's markets for Japan; she was overwhelmed with foreign orders, and she had a completely free hand in the Far East. The victory of the Allies again won for her new territory and greater influence. During the war she had developed a really modern industrial system and had accumulated large capital reserves.

In 1923 earthquake and fire destroyed most of Yokohama and Tokyo, the least industrialized of her large cities. The disaster enabled the Japanese to modernize these cities when they were rebuilt and to make improvements which would otherwise have been impossible. The reconstruction of two of her largest cities created work on a huge scale in Osaka, Kobe, Nagoyas and other industrial centres. Japan's industry was again tremendously stimulated, and this happened at a time when a crisis of over-production was threatening to paralyse her commerce.

The 'Manchurian Incident' of 1931 was the second national emergency, which stimulated industry quite as much as the earthquake had done. The influence of this 'incident' is still felt and will, according to official opinion, reach its climax in 1935–6 in connexion with the naval problem, and the threat of a great war. This stimulus, as on previous occasions, appeared at a time when the people were materially and morally exhausted, and it is driving industry to tremendous, though dangerous, heights of expansion.

The Japanese Government directed industry in each of these eventful situations. To a certain extent industry was called up each time for patriotic service, and controlled by the State. The periods between these national events being short, industry did not grow accustomed to freedom; besides, even during these intervals of rest State control remained strong and stubborn.

In Japan, State and industry did not develop side by side as they did in other countries. When Japan was awakened by foreign guns in 1853, the State, during domestic struggles lasting for decades, first modernized itself, and then began to modernize industry. At the same time it began to produce modern arms and a modern fleet. Japan's governmental machine and her military development were always a few paces ahead of her industry.

It was the State which gradually made 'capitalists' out of a small, heterogeneous, inefficient and not very wealthy group of merchants, feudal lords and unemployed officers, who were instructed to accumulate investment capital and to develop industrial initiative. The State built model factories, banks and railways, and counteracted the lack of activity and experience in the country with subsidies and good advice. The State taxed agriculture so that industry could develop. The State sent suitable men to Western schools and universities, for the great Emperor Meiji had said:

'Knowledge from all parts of the world shall

be made use of so that the State will be made strong and secure.'

Leadership within the State gradually changed. First the Army and the Navy came of age, then finance and industry. The fighting Services and industry, originally creations of the bureaucracy which—with the Imperial authority in the background—had created the new State, gradually became its partners. Both the fighting Services and industrialists gained influence and power, and neither predominated. The civil service, which still likes to indentify itself with the State, has retained influence by mediating between the two powerful and antagonistic interests.

As military ideas could prevail only in war periods, and economic interests normally inclined towards liberalism, the Government's guardianship of industry gradually slackened. But it never disappeared altogether, and as political parties, more or less closely associated with economic interests, came into disrepute, Government interference again increased. It was encouraged by the military circles, whose power has greatly risen since the 'Manchurian Incident' and the opening of the naval discussions.

MOTIVE FORCES BEHIND ECONOMIC POLICIES

This Government interference in commerce and industry resulted from misgivings concerning foreign policies of other countries and from recurring humiliations and dangers, real or imaginary, which Japan met by strengthening and preparing industry for emergencies. It seems necessary to enumerate these emergencies briefly, for in the West there is a habit of seeing only Japan's tremendous military and economic successes, and to think that she ought to be quite content. Japan's failures, which are felt quite as keenly and sincerely as her successes, are often forgotten. Yet these failures are closely connected with her successes; they were, in fact, the price she was forced to pay for her progress.

The enforced opening up of the country gave Japan an opportunity of modernization, but, as a result, Western powers inflicted humiliations on her which she has never forgotten. Some of these, like the demand for extraterritorial rights, and the refusal of customs autonomy, happened within living memory.

Her victory over China was followed by the interference of Russia, France and Germany, who deprived Japan of her most valuable booty, the Liaotung Peninsula, her first foothold on the Asiatic Continent.

Nor could Japan really exploit her victory over Russia, because America intervened. Japan was forced to forgo a war-indemnity as well as a foothold in Manchuria and on Northern Sakhalin.

The Versailles Peace Conference refused to grant to the victorious ally the ardently desired proof of 'race equality': it deprived Japan of the laurels of Shantung won against Germany in China.

The Washington Naval Conference forced Japan to surrender her valuable alliance with England, to leave the Russian territories which she had occupied, and to renounce naval equality.

Japan's most recent international successes, the creation of her foster-state Manchukuo, and her great gains in international trade, are still being challenged.

Japan has always believed that the world was hostile towards her and envious of her progress. And her conviction has grown that the only solution of her difficulties would be expansion on the continent of Asia, in the Pacific, in the whole wealthy world which lies beyond her small over-populated islands.

The ever-threatening deadlock between domestic pressure and outward resistance has been mainly responsible for the breathless pace of Japan's industrial progress, and for the State's far-reaching influence on industry.

Such is the background of State assistance in Japan. It should be realized that Government influence on industry will increase—and may perhaps become absolute control—in proportion as Japan's domestic and foreign difficulties increase.

FEW SUBSIDIES, BUT——

In the West it is often claimed that some Japanese export trades are directly subsidized by the Government. This is not the case.

The Tokyo *Oriental Economist* stated in August 1934: 'The fact should not be overlooked that the advance of our exports is due in a great measure to the concerted efforts of Government and people for many years past.'

What are these 'efforts' of Government?

The subsidies to shipping, amounting to 10,000,000 yen a year, are the only important direct financial subsidies. This shipping subsidy is meant to assist a 'scrap-and-build' policy. Subsidies of this kind are not unusual to-day, and several countries contribute even more generously to their merchant fleet. The Japanese export and import trades, however, undoubtedly derive considerable benefits from these subsidies, which are skilfully allotted.

The young motor-car industry, so important from a military point of view, is subsidized, but not heavily. All other subsidies to industry, which probably amount altogether to less than the shipping subsidy, are granted only in the form of indirect encouragement.

The Japanese Government no longer grants cash allowances to individual industries: nor does it now establish new industries on its own account. To-day Japanese industry can stand on its own feet. Government-owned enterprises are confined to tobacco plants, railway works, &c. Even the large iron and steel works, which were under Government control for decades, and the development of which was the most expensive, the longest and the most disappointing industrial experiment undertaken by the State, have recently been made independent. The Government, however, still retains its share of capital and influence. The natural conditions of the iron and steel industry being as unfavourable as its importance to national defence is great, it continues to enjoy freedom from taxes despite the rise in prices, and in some cases, in profits.

Apart from financial subsidies the Government assists industry by the following means:

In the first place by the tariff policy. High customs duties provide many industries, strong enough to supply home markets, with a more or less complete domestic monopoly; and other industries are at least stimulated to further expansion. These semi-monopolies are particularly effective, as an important part of Japanese home consumption consists of specifically Japanese goods, which are outside international competition. Since 1911, when Japan's customs autonomy was recognized by the Western Powers, import duties, which had been kept at the minimum level, have sharply advanced. Recently the Government was given power to introduce reprisal duties on certain foreign products up to 200 per cent. This method of State assistance, too, is not very different from those applied by other countries.

GOVERNMENT ORDERS

The Japanese Government, furthermore, is an important customer of domestic industries. The relatively low purchasing power of the people is somewhat counteracted by the Government's steady demand for arms and munitions and for commodities needed in public works. The State's influence as a consumer is very great. In this connexion it may be important to know the relative importance to Japanese industry of exports, Government purchases, and private domestic consumption.

'In recent years, more than 20 per cent of the whole manufacturing output has become dependent on foreign consumers,' Mr. Kimura, the Director of the Japanese Chamber of Commerce and Industry, wrote in a magazine article late in 1934; and Dr. Takeuchi, the economist of the Tokyo Chamber of Commerce and Industry, in his book *Export Control*, which was published only in Japanese, places this figure at 22 per cent. Comparing production and export statistics the latter figure seems correct; 93·3 per cent of potteries and porcelain are sold to foreign customers; 76·2 per cent raw silk, 51·6 per cent cotton textiles, 51·5 per cent hosiery, 45 per cent rayon textiles, 19·7 per cent silk textiles, 17 per cent woollen textiles, 33 per cent electric bulbs, &c.

Government purchases of industrial products

can be roughly estimated from the Budget. More than half of the present expenditure is for salaries, pensions, payments of interest on loans, &c. Of the other half, which includes expenditures for arms and munitions, building materials, commodities needed for State railways, &c., between 750,000,000 and 900,000,000 yen are paid annually to domestic industries. This sum would represent between 14 per cent and 16 per cent of the production value of manufacturing industries. The following distribution of sales would therefore result: Government purchases, 14–16 per cent; orders from abroad, 22 per cent; private home consumption, 62–64 per cent.

When, however, the purchasing power of civil servants, soldiers and sailors—all consumers directly dependent upon the State—is taken into consideration, the private domestic market is probably smaller than the above figure would indicate; it may, in fact, absorb less than half the total production. This argument may have taken us out of our way, but it serves as a background for an understanding of present tendencies aiming at a reorganization of Japanese industry on the basis of State Capitalism, which will be discussed in greater detail later.

The importance of the large State orders to Japanese industry, and to the strengthening of her international competitive ability, will be further illustrated by the following quotation from the annual report for 1933 of the Yokohama and Tokyo Foreign Board of Trade: 'In addition to high tariff barriers the Government, when placing orders, gives an absolute preference to home-made goods, regardless of price.' Again, this is by no means a Japanese peculiarity.

LOW TAXES

The Government's financial policy supports industry's international competitive ability. As compared with other countries, industry is not heavily taxed in Japan.

In the first place, even to-day, agricultural taxes are relatively higher than industrial taxes. The Imperial Agricultural Society recently compiled comparative figures, showing the national and provincial taxes imposed on agriculture and on industry. These figures indicate that agricultural taxes on an annual income of 2,000 yen are two and three quarters times as high as the taxes on the same income earned in industry or trade. An agricultural income of 5,000 yen is taxed twice as heavily; and the taxes on one of 100,000 yen are three-quarters higher in agriculture than in industry or trade.

In the second place, in Japan, where the family system prevails, expenditures for social welfare, which are so important in the budgets of Western countries, are almost unknown. Japan is not, furthermore, burdened with war debts, the interest payments on which are the second largest item in Western Government budgets.

And, as has been said, the extraordinary expenditure resulting from the 'Manchurian Incident' and the increase of naval armaments have not been paid by an increase in taxation, but by loans. The two-thirds of the Japanese Budget which are met by ordinary revenue are chiefly derived from indirect taxes, customs duties, the Post Office, railways and monopoly enterprises. Direct taxes, including income, land, business profits, capital interest and inheritance taxes, covered only 14 per cent of Government expenditure in 1934.

This system of taxation is obviously directed quite consciously towards the development of Japan's industry and commerce.

The income tax for individuals is 2 per cent on an annual income of over 1,200 yen. The scale rises gradually to 13 per cent on incomes of over 20,000, 21 per cent on incomes of 100,000, and up to 36 per cent for an annual income of more than 4,000,000 yen.

Corporations pay 5 per cent income tax and 3·4 per cent business profits tax. Besides, an excess profits tax of 4 per cent is paid by corporations with an annual profit of more than 10 per cent of the capital. This tax rises to a maximum of 20 per cent for that proportion of the income which amounts to more than 30 per cent of the capital. The excess profits tax has been increased in the 1935–6 Budget.

The regulations governing the tax-free redemption of fixed capital provide for 'metal machinery ' to be redeemed within twenty-five years, and ' metal tools ' within thirty-five years.

The total annual taxation—State, provincial, municipal—in Japan is about 18 yen per head of the population (£1 16*s*. at par; £1 at the present rate of exchange). That is about one-twentieth of the average British taxation. And this despite the fact that at present Japan is spending, at par, almost as much as Great Britain on her national defence.

GOVERNMENT CREDIT

Already in the early stages of modernization the rapidly expanding private banks helped the State to finance industry. Contrary to British, and similar to German, practice, private banks in Japan were closely—often too closely—connected with industry from the very beginning. The Government organized agricultural and industrial credits by founding and supporting special banks, which provided money for small- and medium-sized enterprises. That was usually done by mortgages, but other methods of credit were introduced as well. To a certain extent the State's special banks restrained the monopolist tendencies of the large private banks.

A number of special banks were organized: the Yokohama Specie Bank, dealing with foreign exchange business; the Hypothec Bank of Japan; the Industrial Bank of Japan; many agricultural and industrial banks; and finally the Central Chest for Industrial Associations. Today deposits in the special banks amount to about one-sixth of the deposits in ordinary banks; the general loans and discounts of the special banks are about two-thirds, and their investments about one-half of those of ordinary banks.

The special banks, the paid-up capital of which is about a third of that of ordinary banks, work largely with capital derived from the issue of bank bonds. Most of the debentures of these banks are in the hands of the 'Deposit Bureau of the Department of Finance', which, with the Bank of Japan, functions as a central bank and deals chiefly with the huge deposits of the Post Office Savings Bank, which the Deposit Bureau controls.

Despite all State support, credit has always been expensive in Japan, because the total capital accumulated has been wanted for industry. Recently, however, Japan's international competitive ability has improved in this field, too. The Government's 'beneficent inflation', which is confined almost entirely to bank credits, has caused money rates to decrease. Call money has cheapened on an average by one-half; discounts by one-fifth; and commercial bank loans by about one-seventh. At the end of 1934 the rates for the last two, however, were still from 5·5 to 6 per cent.

These averages, moreover, conceal very high costs of accommodation for a number of small and some medium-sized industrial enterprises, as well as the extraordinarily high rates for agricultural credits, while often very comfortable rates are granted those large enterprises which are closely associated with large financial concerns or belong to them. The following figures show how expensive credit was for small- and medium-sized enterprises at the end of 1934: A medium-sized private bank demanded 9·85 per cent per annum on loans under 2,000 yen; the semi-official Hypothec Bank of Japan demanded 6·8 per cent for small and medium loans on a mortgage. The semi-official Industrial Bank of Japan asked 7·3 per cent per annum for loans on a mortgage amounting to less than 100,000 yen; and 8 per cent per annum when there was no mortgage. These rates are possible despite the Bank of Japan's official bank rate of 3·65 per cent for commercial bills.

STATE ENCOURAGEMENT OF ORGANIZATION

Two forces are at work reorganizing and amalgamating Japanese industry, which is still divided up into countless competitive enterprises. The first are the great financial concerns, which will be discussed later. The second force is the Government, which is following Germany's example by co-ordinating the many independent small- and medium-sized concerns.

This means that trusts and cartels are being developed simultaneously, and in recent years the State has encouraged the formation of cartels by legislative measures.

Two laws were passed; one affects all important branches of industry, both home and export, the other directs particularly the promotion of export associations.

Nearly 500 industrial associations have been formed under the first Law, including some which have been reorganized and officially recognized. According to the *Oriental Economist* the functions of these associations are as follows:

> Survey of productive facilities of members; designation of raw and partly manufactured materials; production control and price fixing; establishment of co-operative institutions and lending of machinery for lowering production costs; finishing and distribution of products of member-firms on a co-operative basis; co-operative purchases of raw and partly manufactured materials; accommodating operation funds; technical advice regarding business management.

At the end of 1934, sixty-seven organizations were functioning under the Export Guild Law. Some of them include member-firms exporting the same product; others, firms exporting to the same markets; others, both; and their membership consists of varying numbers of large-, small- or medium-sized enterprises. There is, for example, a general 'Bicycle Export Association', a general 'Cotton and Rayon Textiles Export Association', a 'Textile Exporters' Association of Nagoya', an 'Association of Exporters of Cotton Tissues to British India', a 'Japan-

Near East Export Association of Osaka', a 'Japan-Africa Export Association of Osaka', and an 'Association of Exporters of Medicines to Central America'.

The usual aims of these associations are all or some of the following: fixing export quantities or prices according to markets; inspection of export shipment and enforcement of a fair standard of quality; maintenance of agents abroad; investigation of new markets; advising inexperienced exporters; elimination of middle-men causing a reduction of sales prices; negotiating sales for members; or outright buying from members and direct selling to foreign customers. The Bicycle Association has even sent Japanese families as settlers to Borneo, Java and Sumatra, who, apart from their regular trade, act successfully as agents for bicycles.

The system of quotas for each member varies greatly. This is an example: maximum exports and minimum prices for different markets are fixed every quarter. Nine-tenths of the total exports are allotted to the various members in accordance with the percentage amounts they exported during the preceding year. These allotments can, however, be exceeded by 20 per cent, provided a special commission is paid to the association. If the member in question has orders beyond this 20 per cent, he can be granted a further allotment up to the remaining tenth of the total, as far as it is not yet distributed among new members.

Government subsidies are granted to both types of associations. During recent years these subsidies have amounted to several million yen. One of the special purposes of these Government subsidies is 'to cover part of the expenses of foreign agents'.

Both types of association are relieved of all taxes. For both, low interest loans (mostly under 4 per cent) are available in the Deposit Bureau of the Department of Finance and in the special banks. The Government also guarantees loans obtained from the banks for co-operative purposes. It should also be mentioned in this connexion that an Export Indemnity Law makes the Government responsible up to 70 per cent for losses suffered by certain banks as a result of export ventures, especially when they are in countries which are new buyers of Japanese goods. Under this scheme export bills for millions of yens have been discounted by banks.

In both types of associations membership may be declared compulsory by the State. Outsiders can be forced to join and members must follow the decisions of the majority. So far the practical application of these Laws has been rare. At present the Government is not considered very powerful as far as industry is concerned, and within the Government the Department of Commerce and Industry, directly responsible for the application of these Laws, is not very influential. Often the large and powerful concerns or their affiliated companies are the offenders against whom the smaller competitors seek protection. Quarrels within the cartels and other associations are not unusual. Often production quotas are fixed, but in many cases they are not observed, or they displease a number of producers. Often, too, the efforts of the export associations are counteracted by outsiders, who have recently, for instance, tried to manufacture in Corea and to export from there in competition with the associations.

Cartels have nevertheless already benefited a number of industries. The movement is growing and has spread to the medium-sized industries. These associations are quite rightly called *guilds*, and it is not unimportant for their future that guilds have an old and a sound tradition in Japan. The associations would undoubtedly flourish if a 'strong' Government came into power, such as a Government controlled by military interests. The existing Laws need only be more rigidly applied in order to create a corporate economic system.

The development of these associations is not harmful to Japan's international competitors. On the contrary, they usually tend to curtail excessive price cutting, which is as harmful to her competitors as it is to the Japanese themselves. They also furnish a basis for representation in international negotiations on a reasonable regulation of Japan's export competition. Some of these associations, in fact, were organized with such negotiations in view. The Association of

Exporters of Cotton Tissues to British India is an example. If these typically Japanese organizations could stimulate her Western competitors to form similar bodies, world trade might be planned and developed on a more efficient basis.

CHAPTER EIGHT

MITSUI AND OTHERS

JAPAN'S MOST POWERFUL TRUST

ONE enormous concern handles one-half of Japan's exports. Its share in Japanese imports is not much smaller, and it is said that 60–70 per cent of Japan's total trade with the new State of Manchukuo passes through its hands.

This estimate was given us by an authoritative source in Tokyo, but more conservative estimates do not fall far below this figure.

This great power in Japanese economic life is the Mitsui concern, still largely controlled by the Mitsui family. Only in some of their subsidiary firms have the Mitsui offered some shares to the public. They have done so less to acquire capital—for the concern is self-sufficient in almost every way—than to make their enterprises more popular.

The Mitsui concern is the leading power in Japanese export, import and domestic trade. It maintains huge wholesale trade organizations, dealing in all sorts of products, modern department stores, a large merchant fleet, and vast warehouses. More than this, the concern controls a considerable proportion of Japan's bank deposits, and owns large insurance companies, which bring to it funds from all parts of Japan and from foreign countries.

The family gave up their feudal rank and titles about 300 years ago and exchanged a sword and a coat of mail for a yardstick and a pair of scales. They began as small traders and money-changers. When the country was opened up, and a free international exchange of goods began with the Restoration, the Mitsuis were the only family with reserve capital and business experience—even though, judged by present-day standards, they were not really rich in either. The family co-operated with the new State as advisors and creditors. In decades the family repeated, on a vast scale, the process it had taken centuries to build up on a small scale.

The family's retail trade, which had been courageously modernized even during the feudal age, and which to-day is carried on as a relatively modest side-line in huge department stores under the name of Mitsukoshi, became a world combine, with branches in many industrial centres abroad. And modern Japan's largest financial trust developed out of the Mitsuis' money-changing banks, which had consistently refused to finance feudal quarrels, but had supported the imperial Restoration.

Trade and credit, however, are only a factor, and probably not the most important one, in the

Finance Minister, Mr. Takahashi, Japan's "Grand Old Man" of Finance

The Mitsui Bank in Tokyo. The country's most powerful banking and industrial concern

Mitsuis' powerful position. In modern times, the Mitsuis have become the largest individual industrial enterprise in the whole country. They own the largest coal and iron ore mines in Japan as well as enormous heavy industries and armament plants. They own or control shipyards, building firms, engineering factories, electrotechnical works, chemical plants, large forests, paper and artificial silk factories, cement and flour mills, enormous cotton-spinning works, sugar refineries, colonial estates, and plantations. In almost every branch of industry the Mitsui concern is powerfully represented, or controls a large part of the production.

The tremendous Mitsui trade organizations—chiefly the Mitsu Bussan Kaisha, which is predominantly an export organization—supply the concern from without with enormous quantities of goods to be added to its own production. These trade organizations are the reservoirs for all sorts of Japanese products, manufactured in all types of plants. Here the products of modernized Japanese industry meet the goods manufactured in workshops, and those of the smallest home industries. Probably every marketable commodity manufactured in Japan is sold abroad by Mitsui's world organization, and there are few world products imported by Japan which are not distributed by this concern.

Mitsui buys and sells for its own concern ; for competitors ; for export associations, and for the Government. Mitsui is everywhere.

The family concern of Mitsui is organized like a political unit. For centuries it has had its own Constitution, which is periodically revised. Every member of the family, which now consists of 11 main and branch lines, must take the following oath on this Constitution when he comes of age: [1]

> In obedience to the precepts of our forefathers, and in order to strengthen the everlasting ancestral foundation of the families of our House and to expand the enterprises bequeathed by our forefathers, I solemnly vow in the presence of the August Spirits of our ancestors that, as a member of the House of Mitsui, I will observe and follow the regulations handed down in the Constitution of our House, and that I will not wantonly seek to alter them. In witness whereof, I take the oath and affix my signature thereto in the presence of the August Spirits of our ancestors.

MITSUBISHI

The 'State of Mitsui' within the State of Japan, despite its charities, has more enemies than friends in the country. It might not have developed as it has if there had not been another 'billion yen group' to wage a bitter, uncompromising war against it, holding its influence in check. And neither might have been strong enough to overcome public opposition, if there had not been other, lesser, but still important industrial groups preventing them gaining a monopoly.

[1] The translation is that of the Mitsui family.

Mitsui's counterpart is Mitsubishi. Mitsui means ' three wells ' and is a family name, Mitsubishi means ' three diamonds ', and the name was given to the concern during the second half of the last century by its founder, Yatore Iwasaki, who, it is said, wanted to establish a living monument to himself and the two assistants in his first business ventures. The two trade marks, ' three wells ' and ' three diamonds ', compete with each other everywhere in Japan and in many commercial centres of the world. Mitsui is associated with the larger political party of the country, the Seiyukai; whereas Mitsubishi is usually mentioned in connexion with the second largest party, the Minseito. Through these parties, and through other channels, the two concerns exert a great political influence.

Like the Mitsui concern, the Mitsubishi are still largely a family enterprise, but here, too, the Baron Iwasaki's family dynasty remains in the background. In both concerns the ' cabinets ', or ' brain trusts ', of the boards of directors are the real leaders. Often there are men of genius among them, and as powers in their country and in the vast spread of their interests they have no equal in the world. For Mitsubishi, too—though this concern's foreign trade activities are much more limited than those of Mitsui—owns one of the largest banks in Japan which, together with its insurance companies, provides the concern with outside capital. Mitsubishi, too, has enormous interests in mines, heavy industries, and shipping. The concern owns the most important Japanese shipping line, one of the largest in the world—the Nippon Yusen Kaisha. The concern owns engineering, aircraft, glass, paper, electro-technical, sugar, textiles, and many other factories. Besides, it is one of the biggest landowners in Japan.

Sumitomo and Yasada, also family concerns with far-reaching and varied interests, with large banks to finance their enterprises, are the next largest combines. But as neither they nor the other important family concerns are prominent in Japan's foreign trade, it need only be said here that altogether these plutocratic families control half of the financial capital in the country—Mitsui and Mitsubishi about a quarter.

These powerful family concerns are not the only symptom of the trustification of modern Japanese industry. Apart from these vertical organizations, a horizontal concentration of far-reaching interests exists, within which the great families co-operate more or less harmoniously. The banking system is thus controlled by the 'big five'. In the order of their deposits, which do not vary greatly, they are Sumitomo Bank, Daiichi Bank, Yasuda Bank, Mitsui Bank, and Mitsubishi Bank. Within the all-powerful Japan Cotton Spinners' Association five firms control 55 per cent of the bobbins and 47 per cent of the total production. The Japanese artificial silk industry—to-day the second largest in the world—is controlled by 15 large firms united by a cartel. The paper industry is almost completely in the hands of one large concern. In modern industries the trend towards concentration, stimulated by the last crisis, continues to grow. On the other hand, the industries of the 'Old Japan', still split up into many small enterprises, are drawn into this movement through the sale of their products, the purchase of their raw materials and semi-finished products (e.g. yarn), and their credit transactions, all of which are gradually being taken over by fewer and larger concerns. In some cases co-operatives or middlemen even create a direct link with the great trusts.

PROFITS

The smaller a Japanese factory, the more difficult it is for the manufacturer to make a profit on the difference between the production costs and the sales price on foreign markets. He has to pay higher commissions to agents and middlemen, and if he exports directly, the costs of delivery to foreign customers are greater than those of large firms. Among other functions, the export associations try to decrease this difference between the profits of large and small manufacturers. Such an effort is necessary, for the profits in small or medium-sized industries are often so limited that many of these little 'capitalists' are virtually only hard-working labourers or employees, and their 'profits' compare unfavourably with clerks' salaries in Western or even Japanese factories. Unfortunately no figures are available showing the profits of small- and medium-sized industries. Isolated impressions and numerous symptoms, however, indicate that, with a few exceptions, these profits are considerably smaller than those in the modern section of Japanese industry, which are now to be briefly considered.

The Mitsui concern has compiled statistics of profits made during the first six months of 1934 by 1,250 joint stock companies of all branches of industry, showing that the average annual yield was 9·8 per cent. These firms include more than two-thirds of the total capital of all Japanese joint stock companies. Singling out those branches which are relevant to the subject of this book, the following average profits are shown :

	per cent		per cent
Banking	13·2	Rayon	29·0
Commerce	16·9	Machinery and implements	15·3
Shipping	5·2	Glass, ceramics	22·4
Mining	12·7	Paper	14·2
Chemical	12·6		
Spinning and Weaving, general	16·9		

These averages conceal the fact that the profits of a few of the large enterprises are much higher. Let us consider some of these.

In the banking group, the Mitsui Bank's profit was 19·1 per cent ; the Mitsubishi Bank 19·9 per cent; the Sumitomo Bank 23·7 per cent of their respective capital.

The Mitsui Trust Company had a profit of 30·1 per cent; the Mitsubishi Trust Company 17·9 per cent; the Sumitomo Trust Company 26·2 per cent.

In the trading group the Mitsui trading organization and her foreign branches had a profit of 13·3 per cent and the Mitsubishi, which also maintains branches in many foreign countries, of 19·2 per cent.

In the textile group, Kanegafuchi, one of the largest modern cotton concerns, should be mentioned, with a profit of 40·3 per cent; Fukushima, another large cotton concern, with 29·6 per cent; Tokyo Rayon with 42·5 per cent; Kurashiki with 55·4 per cent; Showa Rayon with 67·4 per cent.

The following examples are interesting as record profits in other industries: Toyoda Loom with 28·3 per cent; Japan Dyestuff with 24·9 per cent; Japan Soda with 26·8 per cent; Japan Steel Tube with 49·8 per cent; Nippon Batteries with 37·1 per cent; Mitsui Mining with 17·1 per cent; Mitsubishi Mining with 20·3 per cent.

The export boom alone is not responsible for these high profits, which, in view of the continuous trade boom during recent years, may not yet have reached their peak. In many cases the armament boom has been directly or indirectly responsible for the high profits since the 'Manchurian Incident' and the Naval Crisis.

In judging Japan's future exports, these figures are interesting because they show that in the 'modern section' of Japanese industry, at least, the margin of profit, and thus the sales prices, could be substantially decreased if a growing resistance to Japanese exports should make this necessary. It is probable, furthermore, that the open and secret reserves of the large concerns are being strengthened during the boom. The industrial groups listed above, for instance, distribute on an average only two-thirds of their profits. During the last grave crisis Japanese industries learned to prepare for bad times. They can decrease prices considerably. And the small industries, too, have not yet reached the point where a further decrease would be quite impossible.

CHAPTER NINE

THE STRUGGLE FOR SUPPLIES

FOREIGN SOURCES

ABOUT two-thirds of the raw materials used in the production of Japanese export goods come from foreign countries. Taking Japan's foreign trade statistics as a basis we find that a little more than half of her total exports of finished products are manufactured wholly from foreign raw materials; a quarter are manufactured largely from foreign, and a quarter wholly from domestic raw materials.

About one-fourth of all Japanese products sold on her domestic markets are manufactured from imported raw materials. According to the 'Factory Statistics of the Department of Commerce' for 1932, the last year in which a census was taken, the total raw material consumption was valued at 3,414,000,000 yen; imported foreign raw materials and 'manufactures for further use in manufacturing' were valued at 1,040,000,000 yen, viz. about 30 per cent.

At present about 95 per cent of the amount realized by Japanese exports is spent on the purchase of raw materials and 'manufactures for further use in manufacturing'.

Japan is poor in raw materials. This deficiency which, according to official opinion, delays the industrialization of the country, has become as much a political slogan, as her over-population. Pressure of population and the shortage of raw materials are the basis of Japan's argument in favour of her political and her foreign trade expansion.

To-day the degree of dependence on foreign raw materials is still tolerable, chiefly because so far her imports of foreign foodstuffs have been small. Advanced industrial countries in Europe—Great Britain, Belgium, Germany, &c.—are far more dependent on foreign raw materials than is Japan. Japan, however, has only begun to manufacture modern industrial products for domestic consumption. Though the demand for these goods is not yet general among the masses, the domestic supply of raw materials is being exhausted and foreign raw materials are needed. Future industrialization will be based increasingly on foreign raw materials. Japanese agriculture, too, is approaching her maximum production of foodstuffs. This means that, as the population increases, and as the living standards, still so low in Japan, are raised, the country will become more and more dependent on foreign foodstuffs.

JAPANESE DEFICIENCIES

Japan abounds in only one raw material—raw silk. The purchasing power of her home markets, which consume not more than 10 per cent of the total supply, is very low, and raw silk is therefore not an important raw material as far as Japan is concerned. There are, of course, silk mills in Japan and a certain amount of finished silk material is exported, but the silk export trade cannot be developed on any considerable scale because most countries that can afford a mass consumption of silk goods, import raw silk and manufacture behind the protection of high tariffs.

Until recently the supply of two other raw materials has been sufficient and no marked shortage will occur in the immediate future. These are coal and copper. Despite low wages, however, mining costs have been very high, because the fields are of low grade, the quality of the coal is unsatisfactory, and it is unsuitable for the production of coke which, in turn, is needed in the production of iron. Electrical power, generated from water, supplements the coal as a source of energy, and the electricity supply can be developed; but coal and copper will gradually have to be imported.

There is a shortage of all other raw materials in Japan to-day: timber by 40 per cent at least; spelter by 55 per cent; petroleum by 65 per cent; tin and hemp by 80 per cent; iron ore by 80 per cent. Even when the total smelting capacity of Japan's iron industry is supplemented by adding an adequate quantity of foreign ores there is still a shortage of pig-iron by 30 per cent.

Cotton, wool, rubber, skins, lead and aluminium are practically non-existent in Japan. She must therefore import all these raw materials. England is in a similar position, but she has more coal and iron, though her supply of most other raw materials is even smaller than Japan's. Germany, France, Italy and the smaller industrial countries in Europe, too, import raw materials. Only the United States and Soviet Russia—both powerful neighbours and the only potential enemies of Japan, with whom alone she now compares her own shortcomings—have an unlimited supply of these commodities. China—the chief concern of Japanese policy and the avowed or secret bone of contention between her, Russia and the U.S.A.—may have considerable resources of raw materials which might be developed. But they are not nearly so great as that of Russia or the U.S.A., the outstanding examples of economic self-sufficiency.

THE ECONOMIC ASPECT

The acquisition of raw materials has a political and an economic aspect for all industrial countries, and interesting facts emerge from a study of Japan's present and future development along both lines.

Let us first consider the economic aspect.

So far the competitive ability of Japanese industry has not been hampered by her shortage of cotton, wool, or other raw materials. Under its present economic system the world is nearly always suffering from over-production, and rarely or never from a shortage of goods. The supply of raw materials is therefore sufficient. Most industries manufacture far from the sources of their raw material, for factories are built where labour is good and cheap, where capital is easily available and where the purchasing power of the consumer is high. Even the United States cotton industry has only recently begun to move to the South near the plantations.

Japan's most important competitors, especially in Europe, buy most of their raw materials on the same foreign markets overseas: cotton in the southern states of the U.S.A., British India and Egypt; wool in Australia, New Zealand, South Africa and the Argentine; hides and skins in North and South America; rubber and tin in the Dutch East Indies and the Straits Settlements, &c. 'World prices' are quoted to all customers, and there is not much difference in shipping costs. This means that with regard to raw material purchases Japan enjoys equality with England and most of her other competitors.

Not only that: Japan has been skilful enough to underbid other countries even in the cost of certain raw materials. The *Report of the Cotton Mission*, the 1931 British Economic Mission to the Far East, stated that Japan had lowered the raw material costs of her cotton industry by using a less conservative mixture of various, relatively cheap types and standards of raw cotton. The Report also confirmed that 'even such types of cotton as she buys often pass to her spinners at a lower price (from 3 to 5 per cent) than to mills in other countries, even to mills in the country of origin (U.S.A. and British India)'.

The fact is that about 70 per cent of Japan's total cotton imports are handled by three large concerns—and that is a unique achievement of efficiency in international trade—which also export two-fifths of the various products of the Japanese cotton industry. These firms are therefore directly interested in the competitive ability of the cotton industry, and try to sell the raw cotton to the mills at a price lower than the official American or Indian quotations. They do that by passing on rebates, which they obtain because they are the most important international buyers on the spot, to their customers. By supplying the industry with raw materials at low prices they hope furthermore to increase their own export profits. These firms always cut down agents' commissions as much as possible, whereas in England and other countries numerous large and small commission agents unload their relatively high costs and profits on the mills.

Many other raw materials are bought and supplied cheaply to the finishing industries by means of a similar concentration of the import trade in a few powerful firms who are also interested in exports. This comprehensive system of monopolies is surpassed only by the Government foreign trade control in Soviet Russia. Raw wool imports, for instance, are controlled by six large concerns, which are at the same time actively interested in the export trade of woollen products. Similar conditions prevail in many other industries.

Japanese industry has not, on the other hand, derived any competitive benefit from the fact that—chiefly for reasons of strategy—she has developed her own production of coal, copper, pig-iron and steel. On the contrary, despite low wages, the mining costs of the relatively unproductive Japanese coal mines are very high because of the poor quality of the coal. Copper presents a similar case. The high cost of coal, the high production costs of the low-grade domestic ores and the expensive bulk transport of ores from abroad, are unfavourable to the iron industry. To a certain extent Japan's manufacturing industries have sacrificed their international equality in the prices of their coal, copper and iron supplies to ambitions for greater military security.

A similar development has occurred in the production costs of rice, Japan's most important foodstuff. Despite the extremely low standard of living in country districts, the high cost of rice production generally makes domestic supplies more expensive than foreign cereals. The relatively high cost of coal, iron and copper, and a relatively high price for a popular foodstuff, are of course expenditures which are felt throughout Japanese industry.

A curious situation has thus arisen in Japan: as compared with the situation of her industrial competitors abroad she is better off as far as her imported raw materials are concerned; but she is at a disadvantage in regard to her domestic raw materials. This fact shows how badly she has been treated by nature.

THE SEARCH FOR CHEAP RAW MATERIALS

Does this mean that in modern industry the cost of raw materials continues to be an important competitive factor?

A cotton shirt, sold in a shop for 6*s*., and to the wholesale trade for 4*s*. 6*d*., does not, in all probability, include more than nine-pennyworth of raw cotton and other raw materials, and the rest of the costs are mainly labour and profit. The prices of various types of cotton yarn include up to 70 per cent or 80 per cent of raw material costs, and the prices of unfinished cotton materials still include 50 per cent. In the finished material, however, labour and other production costs outweigh the raw material costs. The cost of raw materials used in the manufacture of a machine sold at £100, or even of a motor-car sold at £200, is not more than the same number of shillings. The more finished a product the smaller is the percentage cost for raw materials in its final price. The raw material costs in optical instruments and other goods requiring highly skilled labour are negligible as compared with the huge outlay for labour and capital, accumulating during the long process of manufacture from the raw material to the finished product. And that is why industries requiring highly skilled labour in the manufacture of their products can be geographically separated from the source of their raw material. It was essential only for these industries to develop near the sources of labour and capital, and near their markets. That is why, furthermore, differences in wages are more important factors of competition than differences in the costs of raw materials. And as far as wages are concerned, Japan is in a far more favourable situation than are her competitors.

Raw material costs are nevertheless an increasingly important consideration for Japanese industry, not only because, as competition grows keener, even the smallest advantage in costs is essential, but above all because an almost revolutionary change is occurring in the relation between the raw material costs and other items included in total production costs.

For as the process of manufacture is mechanized and becomes cheaper (in other words, as the labour costs involved are decreased), the raw material costs again become a relatively more important costing factor. If the labour costs in the production of each shirt or motor are decreased because new labour-saving machines are installed in a plant, the relative costs for machinery and their upkeep must, of course, rise. But the point is that they do not rise to the same extent as labour costs fall, for the success of labour-saving machines depends upon the extent to which they cause a decrease in the total production costs. If this were not the case, no manufacturer would take the risk of investing money in the rationalization of a factory.

The relative rise of raw material costs in Japanese industry since rationalization began, is illustrated by many examples, one of which is particularly typical. From 1928 to 1933 the relative expenditures for materials in the raw silk industry rose from 14 per cent to 28 per cent of the total production costs, while, at the same time, the expenditure for wages decreased from 25 per cent to 12 per cent.

As domestic and international competition is forcing industry to rationalize—and as technical progress and accumulation of investment capital facilitates that development—the wage factor becomes relatively less vital, and the expenditure on raw materials more important, for the competitive ability of industry.

With this important development in mind let us now turn to the political aspect of the question of supplies.

THE POLITICAL ASPECT

As long as a country is more or less dependent on others for her raw materials, there is a danger that one day she will be cut off from her foreign sources of supply. This is particularly true of countries which might, one day, be actively involved in a war. For these countries it would be not only inconvenient but fatal if their imports were to be cut off. Japan is, or thinks that she is, in this precarious situation; and this fact, or this feeling, is not appreciably affected by the fact that she owns iron and coal mines in China, iron mines in Malaya, and rubber plantations in south-eastern Asia, or by the fact that in case of war her mighty fleet would very probably be able to protect many of her trade routes.

That is why Japan has developed her own coal and iron industry despite the economic disadvantages involved. And as industrialization spread, as Japan became an increasingly influential Great Power, her politicians resolved more and more firmly to create an independent domestic source of supplies of raw materials.

Manchuria's separation from China, the creation of the State of Manchukuo and its incorporation in the 'Japanese-Manchurian Economic Bloc' have been brought about largely with this aim in view. One of the outward causes of Japan's action on the 18th September 1931 was the fact that she owned sources of raw materials in Manchuria merely by capital investments, and that these possessions seemed endangered because she did not control Manchuria politically. Japan's action in September 1931 is the most important—though not, perhaps, the best—step she has yet taken towards her economic independence.

MANCHUKUO

Manchukuo's potential wealth of raw materials is not yet accurately known. People say jestingly in Tokyo that the most promising raw material in Manchuria is the air from which an unlimited quantity of nitrogen can be produced. In fact, reports are not very encouraging.

True, there is more iron and coal in Manchukuo than in Japan, but neither is of better quality or cheaper to produce. Above all, they are almost as unsuitable for the heavy industries as are the supplies of the mother country.

Liquid oil hardly exists. Theoretically, of course, it should be possible to produce oil from the Manchurian oil shale, and by hydrogenation of Manchurian coal, but both these processes would involve prohibitive production costs.

It is also doubtful whether the relatively small district which might be climatically suitable to cotton growing would ever produce sufficient cotton at a reasonable cost.

Theoretically, at least, great quantities of wool could be produced in the Mongolian districts belonging to Manchukuo, but before such a plan could be realized the nomadic tribes in Mongolia would have to be persuaded to change the breeds of their sheep so that a quality of wool suitable for industrial purposes could be produced. The tribes are at present resisting these changes which would lower the quality of mutton, their chief foodstuff, and of the skins, their traditional clothing.

After large and expensive transportation schemes have been carried out, plenty of wood for building and for the production of pulp will be available in Manchuria. It is the only raw material which is known to exist there in large quantities, in good quality and in conditions favourable to exploitation. We are not concerned here with the possibilities of increasing agricultural production, but it should be mentioned that if the traditional Japanese rice diet were somewhat changed, Manchurian agriculture could provide more than enough foodstuffs to supply Japan. The development of cattle breeding in Manchukuo, for which conditions are very favourable, might make up for Japan's almost complete lack of skins and leather.

Unless new and important discoveries are made, Manchukuo will provide Japanese industry mainly with such raw materials which, like the domestic coal, copper, and iron reserves, are important politically and strategically, but are a liability rather than an asset in the competitive economic struggle with other countries. Numerous raw materials are lacking in Manchukuo, as in Japan, and as far as one can see, the opening up of Manchuria will not affect the international competitive ability of Japan in the near future. The new country bids fair to be a liability, especially as the expense incurred in the political-military struggle for the supply of raw materials is excessive, and must curtail the amount of money devoted to industry.

But those Japanese enthusiasts who believe in a Manchurian solution of the Japanese problem, the men who actually separated the country from China in 1931, are not foreign trade experts, but militarists. They wanted this province as a Japanese base of defence on the Asiatic mainland, to be incorporated in a huge economic 'bloc' under Japanese rule. These men believe in State Socialism, or State Capitalism; their motives are political and patriotic and they are not interested in profits. They would gladly sacrifice many export advantages, if this would make their country even approximately self-supporting, just as they have already done by the continuous expansion of the heavy industries.

These militarists were, in fact, largely responsible for the Government subsidies to these industries. If the self-sufficiency of the country were strategically satisfactory and provided enough employment, military circles in Japan would not mind a very low living standard throughout the country. They would be glad to see Japan less closely connected with foreign markets. International competition has made many domestic measures, which seem necessary to these men from a military and social point of view, economically unfeasible. Militarists also recognize clearly that to-day Japan is paying far too much, in the products of her cheap labour, for relatively expensive foreign raw materials ; and they would prefer to direct a part of the national energy, now consumed in foreign trade, towards the domestic task of building up the newly created ' Japanese Manchurian Economic Bloc '—prefer it at least until Japan is consolidated on a higher economic and political level, so that the country will not have to beg, bargain and underbid, in international trade.

If Manchukuo's raw materials should prove inadequate for Japan to attain a state of even Spartan self-sufficiency—and those in command will soon see whether this is the case or not—Japanese military circles would probably try to expand the ' Japanese-Manchurian Economic Bloc ' so that it would include potentially wealthier parts of East Asia. Despite the risk and expense involved in such a policy, they would prefer it to falling back entirely on the old commercial solution of the supplies problem : increasing Japanese exports for the sake of financing a continuously rising tide of imports.

POLITICS AND ECONOMICS

It is possible that in the long run only a political step will solve Japan's raw material problem. In 1931 the Japanese Foreign Office defended the country's Manchurian policy to the League of Nations in the following terms: 'Frankly, it is not unreasonable for us to entertain a fear as to whether advanced industrial countries will long continue to supply the materials to our industries which compete with their own.' And in the distant future, it is not impossible that this fear may be well founded. Perhaps the world economic system, so chaotic to-day, may then be consolidated into large, politically stable economic 'blocs', in which the present over-production no longer exists and an organized exchange has been established within each 'bloc' between the producers and the consumers of raw materials. If Japan did not belong to such a 'bloc', her situation would indeed be very serious.

It is our object only to establish two facts.

In the first place: The development of Japan's export trade will depend largely upon the increase or the decrease of the influence exerted by her militarists on national policy.

And in the second place: A political solution of the problem of raw material supplies can hardly satisfy the economic needs of Japanese industry. For a time, at any rate, most of the raw materials acquired by Japan for political reasons must be more expensive than are those for which she can bargain on world markets.

For the present Japan is dependent upon foreign raw materials, and her dependence will become greater the more she invests in Manchuria and the more she prepares for the political struggle for her supplies of raw materials. Her import demands, on the other hand, have always been the chief impetus behind the expansion of her export trade.

CHAPTER TEN

THE FIGHT FOR MARKETS

TOKYO STUDIES THE MAP

THE Japanese are 'export conscious'. The figures of exports and imports, published three times a month, are anxiously discussed by officials, business men, and public opinion. A slight decline in exports over the ten-day period is apt to cause widespread nervousness.

They are observing with growing uneasiness that one foreign country after another is raising obstacles against their exports, until by now the whole range of products is affected by protective tariffs, import quotas, or other trade barriers.

Resistance abroad has not yet done much harm to Japan. She has had to import more, and find new markets for her exports, but the total of exports has risen at a time when the foreign trade of other countries has declined.

But Japan is thinking of the future. Pressure is growing within the country, and, for all her efforts, the export markets are being narrowed down by barriers which must ultimately become effective.

So Tokyo is studying the map of the world to find a way out. Nowhere are maps seen so frequently on office walls, or under glass on the desk.

Seen from here, the small curve of islands in the East, facing the great Asiatic-European mainland—Nippon, coloured red, is the centre of the world. Where are its markets?

The British Empire is fast raising barriers against the rising flood of Japanese exports. The Soviet Union is tending towards economic self-sufficiency. The United States sells more to Japan than she buys from her.

There is China, industrially and physically undernourished. She may ultimately become Japan's most important market, but in the immediate future political hostility and the influence of the Western powers are difficult to overcome.

South of China lie wealthy tropical countries, the Philippines, the Dutch East Indies, the Straits Settlements, &c., potentially even better markets and sources of raw materials than they are at present; these countries, governed by foreign industrial powers, show a growing resistance to Japan's increasing exports.

Where the colours of the Great Powers fade begin new lands of promise: some in Africa, a few in Asia, many in Central and South America. But these new markets, too, have old and established trade connexions; they, too, resist new exporters who are not, at the same time, purchasers of their own products. And these new markets export goods for which Japan has little use: coffee and meat, grain and copra. Here again, Japanese exports may soon find more problems than hope.

Therefore Japan concentrates her attention on countries which she has either conquered or which she controls. Formosa and Corea are themselves in need of more export markets, and cannot become large importers of Japanese goods. Economically their conquest has not profited Japan. Kwantung, the Japanese outpost towards Manchukuo, and finally Manchukuo itself are long-term investments which may one day pay for themselves, but which cannot for many years to come take the place of foreign markets which pay for Japanese exports in the usual way. Indeed, Manchukuo represents another reason why Japan must gain more world markets so that she will be able to meet the tasks awaiting her in this new State.

In vain the anxious foreign trade experts study the world map again and again. Nowhere do they find a real solution of Japan's growing problems. The map, in fact, leaves them no way but to grasp every political and economic opportunity, and to fight and press forward wherever they can.

What has Japan actually achieved by her struggle to win world markets?

COMPETITIVE GOODS

To-day Japan exports five or six times as many finished products as she did in 1914. If the exports of 1914 are used as a basic index of 100, the quantitative development of her exports is as follows:

1914, 100; 1920, 210; 1928, 254; 1932, 325; 1934, 555.

Japan's quantitative share in the world's trade of manufactures is now almost 10 per cent.

In some products her share is much larger; in cotton tissues, for instance, it is 40 per cent. Even the average figure is lower only than the shares of the four industrial Great Powers: Great Britain, the United States, Germany and France, which together monopolize two-thirds of this world trade.

Using the Bank of Japan's *Index of Wholesale Prices* to eliminate the changes in the price level it can be calculated that the total value of Japan's exports in 1934 was three and a half times as great though the volume was only two and a half times as much as in 1914. Altogether Japan's total exports represent only 3 per cent of world exports. Both figures, however, are misleading, if, as is often done, they are used to measure the international importance of Japan's exports. For such comparisons do not take note of the difference between competitive and non-competitive goods.

Raw silk, for example, once Japan's chief

export, and still the second largest item on her export list, is not a competitive article for most industrial countries ; nor are menthol and other typically Japanese products objects of competition.

Cotton goods, artificial silk, bicycles, pencils, and other Japanese industrial products, on the other hand, are highly competitive. These products are becoming increasingly important in Japan's exports, whereas silk, camphor, &c., are less so than they were. Non-competitive goods must be eliminated, in order to make it clear that the relatively slow rise of total exports conceals a far greater success in the field of manufactured goods.

In a comparison of Japanese exports with the total exports of other countries only comparable goods can be used : grain, other foodstuffs and raw materials, for instance, the most important items in world trade, cannot be compared with manufactured goods, the largest item in Japanese exports. Japanese exports of competitive goods must be compared with world exports of competitive goods.

A comparison of the value of these goods, even in gold, would be equally misleading, for in many cases the prices of competitive Japanese goods are lower than the prices of such goods produced elsewhere. For a thousand million square yards of Japanese cotton cloth represent a fifth of the world trade in cotton tissues as accurately as a thousand million square yards of the English material, even though the latter is considerably more expensive than the Japanese product. The true picture can only be revealed by a comparison of quantities.

On these grounds we have, by way of approximate calculations, reached conclusions which may well destroy the illusion that 'Japanese exports are not very important'.

Industrially competitive goods (by this we mean all those goods quoted in the Japanese Trade statistics as in addition to cotton yarn, wheat flour, refined sugar, beer and tinned foodstuffs) are now an increasingly important item in Japan's total exports, particularly during recent years. In 1928 these goods represented only about half of her total exports; in 1934 they represented nearly three-quarters; and the total itself had risen considerably. Japan's rapid industrialization and the sharp drop in the price of raw silk, her non-competitive staple commodity, have been important factors in this development.

Textiles still head the list of Japanese exports of competitive goods, and cotton tissues are the chief item among textiles.

To-day Japan is the largest exporter of cotton tissues in the world; her share of 40 per cent is larger than that of Great Britain. The British record, established shortly before the war, was 7,000,000,000 square yards of cotton tissues. At that time Japan was not a serious competitor. A few figures will illustrate the later development of British and Japanese exports of cotton tissues (in million yards):

	Great Britain.	Japan.
1928	3,866	1,419
1932	2,198	2,032
1934	1,995	2,568

Great Britain's exports of cotton tissues have gone back to the figures of the 'sixties, the time when feudal Japan was opened to international trade by force. At that time Japan had hardly any industry worth the name, and Japanese pioneers were coming to England to study Western spinning methods. And to-day Japan is ahead of Great Britain by 500,000,000 square yards!

True, total world trade in cotton goods has decreased because of the depression and because domestic cotton industries have developed in countries which were formerly important customers. And Lancashire, in many ways so backward, has lost far more export trade than progressive Osaka has gained.

Japan's artificial silk exports—and Japan has been producing this commodity for only a few years—have also gone beyond Great Britain's figure. Since 1933 Japan has been the second largest producer of artificial silk—immediately behind the United States.

In 1930–2 Japan's young woollen industry exported only 2·5 million yen worth of cloth; in 1934 this figure represented the average of monthly exports. The exports of all other textiles—knitted goods, shirts, underwear, &c.—have risen by more than half during the same period.

Japan began her career on world markets as a simple exporter of raw silk. During the second phase of her development as an exporter, cotton tissues seemed the only item which could be added. Soon, however, in the third phase, she became a leading exporter of artificial silk and of other textiles. And already the fourth phase has begun, for of late the exports of all textile products have been exceeded by the exports of non-textile 'general industrial merchandise'.

This sensational development occurred in 1934. In 1932 'non-textiles' represented only 37 per cent of Japan's total exports of competitive manufactured articles; in 1933, when both textile and total exports rose sharply, 'non-textile' were 41 per cent; and in 1934, when exports as a whole had again risen, 'non-textiles' were 46 per cent. Japan has become an all-round exporter of industrial products. Textiles are no longer her chief export item.

The 'non-textiles' which Japan to-day exports up to a value of at least £1,000,000 each include the following: tinned foodstuffs; wheat flour; refined sugar; drugs and chemicals; dyes, paints, &c.; boots and shoes; buttons and jewellery; paper; potteries; glass and glass-ware; iron rails; enamelled ware, cutlery and nails; clocks and scientific instruments; lamps; toys.

In 1934 the exports of all of these non-textile manufactures were two and a half times as high as Japan's total imports of wholly manufactured articles; while in 1932 they were only twice as high as these imports. Japan's excess of production in almost every branch of industry, a development which began only a few years ago, is rapidly increasing.

BRITISH EMPIRE MARKETS

In 1933, the last year for which detailed statistics are available, the British Empire imported 35·5 per cent of all Japanese exports of competitive industrial manufactures. With 1914 as a basis of 100, the volume of all Japanese exports to the British Empire rose to 180 in 1925, to 300 in 1933, and to about 428 in 1934.

If the exports to the leased territory of Kwantung and to Manchukuo are excluded, Japan's exports of competitive industrial manufactures were distributed as follows in 1933: British Empire, 44·6 per cent; Dutch Empire, 16·0 per cent; U.S.A. markets, 12·8 per cent; China (excluding Manchukuo), 9·0 per cent; rest of the world, 17·6 per cent.

Provisional figures for 1934 indicate little change in the proportions taken by these markets. Great Britain herself imports only a tenth of the competitive industrial articles exported by Japan to the British Empire. In 1934 Great Britain imported the following goods to the value of three to four million pounds each: tinned food, shirtings, striped drills, towels, silk tissues, artificial silk tissues, knitted goods, shirts and under-shirts, hats, buttons, paper, potteries, glass, brushes, electric lamps, toys, rubber and other boots, enamelled ware, bicycles, celluloid ware, pencils, rubber goods, &c.

Great Britain imports, however, more than half of Japan's relatively small non-competitive exports to the British Empire. These are: raw silk; plaits for hat making; camphor, wood, &c., and their imports into Great Britain are each valued at about two to three million pounds a year.

In common with many other industrial countries, Great Britain is not yet faced with really keen competition with Japan on her home markets; for the cheap Japanese goods are sold mainly to low-standard countries, where they compete with exports from England and other countries. In 1934, 83 per cent of Japan's industrially competitive goods were exported to low-standard countries, and only 17 per cent to countries with a modern standard of life.

Australia, New Zealand and Canada, typically high-standard countries, import only another tenth of these Japanese exports, about as much as Great Britain herself.

British India, a typically low-standard country, imports about half of the remaining Empire share of Japanese exports, to the value of over £12,000,000 a year. The other half is almost equally divided between the African countries in the British Empire—Egypt, South Africa, and the Colonies—and the Asiatic group comprising the Straits Settlements, Hongkong, Ceylon, British Borneo, Iraq, Palestine and Aden. All types of Japanese goods are exported to these countries, but the chief item is, of course, cotton tissues.

At first glance Japan's commercial position on British Empire markets as a whole appears to be relatively strong, because she imports more goods from the Empire than she exports to it. In 1933 the difference in Great Britain's favour amounted to almost 20 per cent; in 1934 it was still some 6·5 of Japan's exports. The relation between Japanese exports and imports to and from various individual countries in the British Empire, however, has recently been in Japan's favour. This is true of Japan's trade with Great Britain, and with the African and Near Eastern countries in the Empire. Japan's trade balance with Canada, Australia, New Zealand and Borneo, on the other hand—countries which all export raw materials to Japan and import only small quantities of goods—was unfavourable to Japan. And the Agreement of 1934, which will be mentioned later, has caused Japan's trade balance with British India to be in the latter's favour.

Japan's dilemma in connexion with her trade with the British Empire is typical of her position in world trade: though she imports more than she exports, she is unable to use this fact to protect her rising exports. For her most important customers and her most important sources of supplies are not, as a rule, identical. To-day, however, most countries tend to buy no more from a certain country than it will buy from them, and 'reciprocity' has become the chief problem of Japan's trade policy. She has to solve this problem partly by meeting reciprocity demands and partly by bargaining for reciprocity herself.

TRADE DISARMAMENT

British India and the Dutch East Indies have been most determined in resisting Japanese trade expansion. These countries are the largest single buyers of Japanese manufactured articles outside the Japanese-Manchurian Empire. In both countries Japanese goods replaced the goods of the Mother Country and other established suppliers, particularly cotton yarn. In British India Japanese cotton imports created a special problem by competing with the domestic cotton industry.

In 1932, apart from other exports into British India, Japan, with 640,000,000 square yards of cotton tissues, had made unprecedented inroads on British Indian markets. The answer was an increase of Indian duties on cotton cloth imports to 75 per cent. Protracted negotiations with British India were begun, which finally, early in 1934, resulted in a kind of economic disarmament agreement. This Agreement, confined to cotton, will expire on March 31, 1937, and new negotiations will have to begin before long. The Indian-Japanese struggle at Delhi is therefore of more than historical importance.

Japan had two weapons in this struggle: the first, India's dependence on Japan as a purchaser of her raw cotton, was stubbornly exploited by Osaka industrialists in the form of a boycott against the Indian raw material. The other weapon was the real or imaginary popular approval in India of the cheaper Japanese cotton tissues. The Japanese, though tacitly counting on this approval, knew better than to exploit openly the words attributed to the then Minister of War, Araki, that Japan could not tolerate a 'white oppression' in India or elsewhere in Asia.

The Agreement fixes maximum exports of Japanese cotton tissues at 400,000,000 square yards, to be distributed amongst various kinds of cloth. Japan can export this maximum into India on condition that she has purchased of India, during the corresponding cotton season, 1·5 million bales of raw cotton. Japanese exports are to be decreased according to an elaborate scale if she imports a smaller quantity of raw cotton. At the same time the Indian import duty was decreased to 50 per cent, with a 25 per cent preference for British goods.

So far Japan has made full use of this Agreement, but, although she lowered her cotton exports to India by one-third, her total exports to that country have continued to rise. The dependence of the Indian cotton planters on Japan has not decreased; and they are still neglected by the British cotton industry, which buys chiefly the American raw material. It is probable, therefore, that a fresh struggle will begin. The prevalent feeling between Japan and Great Britain, or the Empire, will have much influence on Japan's attitude at the next Indian cotton conference.

Tokyo has been less obliging towards the Dutch East Indies, for they are in a less favourable 'give-and-take' position than is British India. In this case Japan has been much franker in exploiting the native population's real or imaginary approval of Japanese imports. The Dutch have, however, been even more stubborn than the Indians and the British in the negotiations resulting from the increase of Japanese exports into the East Indies. They also oppose Japan's competitive shipping lines, and the presence of her wholesalers and retailers on Dutch East Indian markets.

The Dutch Government has, however, had more reason to consider the native population, which is feeling the depression even more keenly and for which cheap Japanese imports have been a blessing. The unusual—and symptomatic—situation arose that, during the negotiations in Batavia, Japan achieved a partial success by boycotting the Dutch East Indies—not by refusing imports from there, but by refusing to supply cheap Japanese pottery, dyed cotton sarongs, and unbleached cotton. This happened at a conference convened to curtail Japanese exports! The negotiations were often highly political, reflecting racial differences, and the Japanese press frequently used phrases not unlike that attributed to General Araki.

After the Delhi negotiations, and after long preparations, a method of extending commercial disarmament was finally discussed in London. But these negotiations were a failure, because the British suggested curtailing the competition in artificial silk as well as cotton tissues on world markets in general; while Japan refused to discuss anything but the sale of cotton tissues on the relatively unimportant markets of Great Britain and the Crown Colonies. Finally, in the spring of 1934, it was decided to impose quotas on the import of cotton tissues into most of the British Crown Colonies. Japan alone was affected by the quotas, and her cotton exports to these countries were halved. These restrictions, which were accepted after some protests, resulted in an increase of exports of other goods to the British Colonies. Total Japanese exports of cotton goods, furthermore, continued to rise during 1934, while British exports decreased further.

Though Japan and Great Britain were not involved in an actual trade war early in 1935, their relations were troubled. The need for some understanding became very urgent.

SELLING SILK AGAINST COTTON

The trade between Japan and the United States consists chiefly in an exchange of Japanese raw silk for American raw cotton. Trade in the former, a luxury article in the U.S.A., was seriously affected by the depression. The latter is of prime necessity for Japan. The price of raw silk depends almost entirely upon the American demand, as the U.S.A. purchase about 90 per cent of Japan's total raw silk exports ; and prices have dropped sharply. The price of raw cotton, on the other hand, a commodity imported by many countries, has shown a far smaller decline. This means that the conditions of this barter trade have recently been very unfavourable to Japan.

From 1921 to 1927 Japan exchanged on an average 1 pound of raw silk for slightly more than 30 pounds of American raw cotton. In 1932 she received only 20 pounds of cotton for 1 pound of her raw silk, and in 1934 only 9 pounds of cotton for 1 pound of raw silk. Formerly Japan had not only paid for most of her raw cotton imports by selling raw silk to the U.S.A. but had a considerable surplus to sell for cash. In 1934 this was reversed : Japan's sales of raw silk to the U.S.A. were only about half the value of her own increased demand for American raw cotton.

That is the Japanese-American trade problem in a nutshell. Japan's situation is actually worse, for, apart from raw cotton, she must import other necessary raw materials from the U.S.A., while the U.S.A. needs relatively few Japanese goods apart from raw silk. In 1934 Japan had an adverse trade balance with the U.S.A. of 370,000,000 yen, though until recently it had always been in favour of Japan. But from what has been said it will be clear that in any trade negotiations with the U.S.A. Japan's position would be hopeless.

Only a rise of raw silk prices, which have been extremely low for many years, could change Japan's unfavourable trade balance with the U.S.A., which is one of the secondary reasons for Japan's export drive on world markets.

There is another reason why low prices for raw silk are closely connected with the increase of Japanese export competition: two of the five million Japanese peasant families breed silkworms, either as a full-time occupation, or to supplement their recurring losses from rice farming. The fall in raw silk prices has meant terrible poverty for these farmers, who, without profits, cultivate the mulberry trees so that the 'honourable silk worms' should be fed by night and day. Much of the surplus labour which is depressing the level of wages belongs to this farmer class.

If the depression continues, and if a further improvement of artificial silk adversely affects the demand for raw silk, Japanese silk culture will gradually be restricted, and both the decrease in wages and the further industrialization of the country will be stimulated.

NEW MARKETS

With the growing domestic pressure of industrialization, and with increasing resistance of established markets to Japanese exports, small and large Japanese exporters, as well as the resourceful Japanese Press, have begun to direct their attention to so-called 'new markets'.

The Government supports these efforts. Expeditions of investigation or propaganda are sent to the far corners of the globe, and foreign visitors and diplomats from politically unimportant countries are received with studied courtesy in Japan. Japan's international political prestige is growing, and these countries, some of which do not feel quite comfortable under the influence of another Great Power, sometimes return these courtesies most graciously—perhaps harbouring certain political hopes.

The success of such efforts to win new markets is clearly reflected by the figures of exports to what the statistics, after mentioning sixty-eight countries by name, calls 'other' countries. In 1932 'others' imported an average of 2,000,000 yen worth of Japanese goods every month; in 1933 this figure had risen to a little over 5,000,000 yen, and in 1934 it was almost 12,000,000 yen. In 1932, on the other hand, Japan imported from them a monthly average of goods valued at only half a million yen; in 1933 the figure was 1,000,000 yen; and in 1934 not quite 2,000,000 yen.

These 'others' are, therefore, becoming less anonymous as far as Japan is concerned, for they are beginning to demand reciprocity or at least greater Japanese purchases of their own goods in return. It is typical that the small State of San Salvador, for instance, after a brief honeymoon of friendship with powerful Japan, has now raised a higher tariff wall against Japanese imports than has any other country, because trade between the unequal partners became dangerously one-sided. The same development is occurring all over Latin America and in many other small countries; for Japan's intentions to stimulate cotton plantation and wool growing in these regions by delivery contracts in order to develop the new markets and to emancipate herself from the U.S.A., Australia, &c., have not yet been carried out in a single case.

Japan undoubtedly performs pioneer work in many of her new export markets and in many low-standard countries as well, for her cheap goods are reaching classes of consumers who formerly could not buy any modern products at all. Japan thus prepares the way for the products of other countries, who often, following Japan's lead, become interested in exporting articles which they had previously neglected. A report of the Nairobi correspondent of *The Times* is symptomatic of this development. He writes that 'medical officers in Tanganyika declare that the purchase of cheap Japanese rubber shoes has done more to prevent hookworm disease than all the efforts of the health department'. That the Japanese are fully conscious of this function of their export activities is shown by the following passage quoted by *Osaka Mainichi* from the report of a Japanese export expedition to Africa: 'To enable these naked people to put on clothes, and to enable them to replace coconut tableware with enamelled ware and porcelain ware made in Japan may perhaps be a responsibility to be shouldered by the Japanese.'

Such thoughts soon lead to political considerations. Again two quotations from the *Osaka Mainichi* will illustrate our point:

> While we were trading at Lagos, the seaport of Nigeria, the customs collectors were unreserved in their praise of Japanese merchandise. The native traders were condemning what they called the merciless way in which they were exploited by the ruling British. You can readily understand they have no use for import restrictions;

and the second:

> When on May 7, 1934, the mother country, England, compelled her colonies forcibly to adopt a quota system, and thus used pressure against Japanese goods . . . Ceylon seethed with anti-British movements. Boycott of British goods was resolved upon and the feeling of 'standing together with Japan' permeated the atmosphere.

CHINA AND MANCHUKUO

Japan has always considered China as her 'natural market', and the world's resistance to her exports has made her particularly aware of China's existence.

The chaotic conditions prevailing in China make her a narrow market in relation to her large population and her huge area. China's foreign and domestic trade in modern industrial products is still confined to the towns on the coast and along the shores of the Yangtse.

Even if China's total import demands were supplied by Japan, this would represent only half of Japan's total exports. Besides, Chinese imports consist largely of raw materials and foodstuffs, which Japan cannot supply. A theoretical Japanese foreign trade monopoly in China would, therefore, only absorb a third of Japan's total exports, unless China were to be developed on a large scale by costly investments of capital.

At present, Japan must share exports into China with other countries. The U.S.A., which supply industrial machinery as well as raw materials and foodstuffs, export to China twice as much as Japan. Great Britain is also ahead of Japan on the list, and Germany is not far behind.

Domestic Chinese industries, furthermore, are becoming increasingly formidable rivals of Japanese exporters on Chinese markets. Chinese industries are growing in the large cities and along the Coast, where districts are unaffected by Civil War and other disturbances. From the employers' point of view wage conditions in China are more favourable still than they are in Japan. Japanese capital, especially in the textile industry, is stimulating this development.

To-day China buys only about 7 per cent of Japan's total exports; that is to say, she takes less than the group of small, new markets designated merely as 'others' in Japanese trade statistics. Japan's share in Chinese imports does not appear to be much larger, even if deliveries by way of the British port of Hongkong are taken into consideration.

Japan's political attitude towards China is the chief reason for her small exports to that country. True, the boycott movement is not as strong as it was; people are tired of it, and Japanese pressure on Nanking is taking effect. Still, Japan's average monthly exports to China proper are now only half as large as they were in 1930, before the 'Manchurian Incident'.

But the high price of silver and the trade depression are even greater factors than the dislike of Japan. The aim of Japan's foreign policy is to conquer this prejudice, to develop economic co-operation with China and eventually to create an economic 'bloc' comprising Japan, China and Manchukuo.

To a certain extent Manchukuo has compensated Japan for her losses in China. Including all the present and former Chinese territories as a basis of calculation—China proper, Manchukuo, and Kwantung leased territory, important for both countries as a trade centre—Japanese exports from 1930 to 1934 have increased by half—a rise equal to that in Japan's total world exports. Trade with China has changed, however, and exports against cash have largely been replaced by exports for investment. The continuation of this trade depends upon Japan's ability to repeat such investments; and upon the rapidity and extent to which present investments begin to yield returns. In other words it depends upon whether or not Manchukuo will become a going concern. Naturally, Japan controls the majority of total imports into Manchukuo, which, stimulated by Japanese investments, represent about a third of China proper's total imports.

Japan, with her dependency Corea, supplies more than two-thirds of all Manchurian imports. Japan and Corea, on the other hand, purchase only about half of Manchuria's exports. As a result the Manchurian trade balance has become 'passive'. Japan will not always be able or willing to finance this deficit with credits. She will probably be forced, after organizing an 'economic bloc' with Manchukuo, to find more world markets, not only for her own chiefly industrial products, but also for Manchukuo's agricultural products. Manchukuo, like Corea, may develop into a liability instead of an asset for Japanese exporters.

Despite the economic alliance with Manchukuo, or perhaps because of it, Japan must continue her fight for world markets with renewed vigour.

CHAPTER ELEVEN

HISTORY MADE IN JAPAN

ORIENTAL EFFICIENCY

IF world trade were not restricted by tariff walls and import quotas, by exchange regulations and boycotts, Japan might become the largest exporter in the world—and in a very short time. She is perhaps the only country of which this is true to-day. The international commerce of other countries might not be appreciably affected by unrestricted foreign trade; Japan, on the other hand, would probably become predominant.

That seems to be one of the most important conclusions reached from a consideration of Japan's present competitive ability. It is a theoretical conclusion for world trade is far from being unrestricted. But it is nevertheless symptomatic of Japan's tremendous progress, which first occurred unobtrusively and later in the glaring light of world publicity. It also explains her attitude towards the restrictions imposed on her export trade by other countries.

To-day Japan is able to manufacture increasing quantities of practically every kind of finished product. Apart from many large factories which are technically the most modern in the world, she possesses a rationalized medium-sized industry, and a mass of small and home industries which are unrivalled in their field, and are not yet producing to anything like capacity.

Japan has already shown that she has an inventive spirit. She is, for instance, proud of her Toyoda looms now being used in Lancashire. So far the list of her patents is small, but it is growing, and Japan will undoubtedly develop her inventive spirit when she has absorbed what she has learned so quickly; when her family system, so neglectful of individual initiative, has been modified; and when she has reformed her script, which is so complicated that it takes years, which youth can ill spare, to master it.

Japan's large working population can be efficiently employed in various types of factories. Her wage level, though far lower than that maintained in other well-organized industrial countries, is by no means an index of her civilization.

Japan has adjusted the external value of the yen, which was too high, to its lower domestic value. Unless her currency gets out of control, there is no reason why Japan should lose her exchange advantage over her competitors.

To-day the State and the large concerns are co-operating in foreign trade promotion, and if the State became stronger than private business —for instance by an increase of the Army's political influence—it would strengthen rather than weaken Japan's competitive ability on world markets. For such a development might bring Japan nearer to a system of planned economy.

One might call the impressive achievements of Japan's industries and foreign trade the first great display of Oriental efficiency. We use the world 'Oriental' not only as a geographical term, but also to characterize the peculiarities of Japanese efficiency, including its numerous shortcomings, gaps, and contradictions.

Particularly 'Oriental' is Japan's social system in which her population is rising to modern efficiency: the long hours of work, the semi-feudal organization, and the Oriental frugality.

Japanese trade methods, too, are very different from those in the West, where even those of large modernized Japanese concerns would often, and quite rightly, be considered clumsy, primitive, wasteful in time and words, casual and unsystematic.

Graft and corrupt practices, in business as in politics, are probably not less extensive than in certain Western countries. Japan is, above all, a country of contradictions. Against her assets of tradition, modernization, human qualities and institutions one must place corresponding drawbacks which impede her progress. It is sometimes surprising that Japan has expanded her markets despite these defects in her trading methods. The achievements of Japan's curious combination of such 'Oriental' characteristics and efficiency are all the more admirable in view of the extraordinary lack of eagerness in the salesmanship of the average Japanese, the time it takes him to perform the simplest task, the difficulties he has with Western languages and habits of thought, the daily struggle of most civil servants, business men and employees to add, subtract, multiply and divide figures. Japanese education is progressive, however; gradually 'Oriental' efficiency will turn into real efficiency, and this development will considerably increase Japan's competitive ability.

THE VERY LONG VIEW

If one takes the very long view, Japan's recent progress is an event of the greatest historical importance, the beginning of a new epoch in the industrialization of the world.

This development will continue not only in Japan; her progress will also encourage other Oriental countries to change from purely agricultural producers to industrial manufacturers.

Japan is already stimulating China's industrialization. She is now, for instance, importing some of the cotton yarns she needs from China although only a short time ago she was still manufacturing and exporting these yarns. She is, furthermore, importing from China rising quantities of unbleached cotton tissues which are finished in her modern factories.

Japan may one day become the industrializing exporter of the East, just as England was in the West. And in the not too distant future Japan may be affected by China and her cheaper labour, even as England is suffering from Japan's competition to-day.

We cannot tell when this will happen, or how it will react on the West. It seems certain, however, that Asia, the most densely populated part of the world, will one day have a tremendous industry, which will fight for expansion not only on her own but on foreign markets as well. Japan is to-day reminding the world of this inevitable development, and she herself will probably play an important part in the industrialized Asia of the future.

THE SHORT VIEW

Such a development may be very slow, though changes are occurring very quickly in Asia.

Japan in the meantime is exposed to many dangers.

Though her great but distant future as an industrial exporter seems to be assured, the next stages of Japan's destiny will be difficult.

An important war, in which Japan would participate with all her strength, is one of the possibilities she is seriously considering to-day. While such a war lasted, Japan would probably cease exporting industrial products. On the contrary, a war would force her to import heavily, and her industry would be reorganized to meet war-time demands.

Even in case of a victory it would be difficult for Japan to recapture her neglected markets quickly, for other exporters, following her own policy during the Great War, would have invaded these markets.

For geographical reasons, it seems out of the question that Japan would be able to conquer any developed, financially sound territory in the immediate future. And it would mean a liability rather than an asset for her to make any further conquests of undeveloped areas such as Manchuria. For military reasons such an expansion would again demand from the impecunious Mother Country heavy investments which could not at once—if at all—be expected to give a financial return. Such further expansion would overtax Japan's financial strength and endanger her economic progress. To-day, even victorious wars are usually an economic loss to the victor, and a defeat would have unthinkable consequences to this highly strung people.

Therefore, whether a war ended in defeat or victory, it would retard Japan's great industrial future; war would not overcome but intensify her crisis.

In a second European war, on the other hand, Japan could act as an observer and an exporter, and she would make tremendous strides towards a predominant position in international trade.

Japan must take into consideration the danger

of her financial policy leading to a real inflation. A drastic devaluation of the yen might not be altogether harmful, because it would also cause a redistribution of wealth, now desired by social reformers in Japan, which would be difficult to achieve by political means. Apart from the Government, the farmers and the owners of small and medium-sized industries are the largest group of debtors in Japan. Big business is the largest creditor. In Germany the inflation impoverished the middle classes and relieved big industrialists of their debts, but in Japan an inflation might benefit the people. On the other hand, agricultural debts in Japan consist largely of liabilities in kind—for instance, 50 per cent of the rice harvest constitutes the land rent. Such debts would not be affected by an inflation. Other specifically Japanese conditions would also limit the wholesome effects of an inflation and enhance its harmful effects.

It is true, however, that a far-reaching event like an inflation might give the social reformers, i.e. certain military circles, an opportunity of bringing about a thorough agricultural reform and a rehabilitation of the middle classes. Such an opportunity would not come their way so easily in normal times.

The end of Japan's present armament boom might also affect her industrial future. It is based on State borrowing and cannot continue indefinitely. It is generally expected that it will cease after the peaceful passing of the so-called 'national emergency of 1935–6'. When the armament boom is over the chronic economic depression will become more acute, unless, by that time, agricultural reform has been started; unless domestic markets have revived; and unless a far-reaching world prosperity has greatly increased the demand for her export goods. Whatever happens, it seems certain that the end of the armament boom will cause increased export pressure. Because of urgent armament orders some firms—for instance dockyards—have recently rejected orders from abroad; for the same reason others have not concentrated on their export trade as they would have done in normal times. An end of the armament boom would show the way to the export markets to numerous branches of Japanese industry which have not yet found that opportunity, although they are technically able to do so.

THE ARMY AND THE FUTURE

Japan's Army is the least-known factor in her future development. What does the Army want? What will it do?

Military circles—and the Navy should be included in these considerations, as the common interests of the Services are usually stronger than their rivalries—have always been more or less influential behind the scenes of politics, and their influence has greatly increased since the 'Manchurian Incident' and the revival of the naval problem. Since the suppression of all left-wing seditious movements, and since the last, apparently final failure of the present parliamentary parties, the fighting Services have become the centre of the radical and progressive movements in the country. Army and Navy accumulate the voices of discontent, and put them before the public. More and more the Services, or at least the reformer elements in them, regard this function as the foundation of their growing power in home politics.

In this anxiety about economic problems the Services are true to military interests, for they consider the discontent and its remedies from the point of view of national defence. They are becoming more familiar with economic problems, more and more eager to find solutions for them. They frequently participate now in economic discussions and might, one day, play a more active part. For naturally they believe that social and economic questions are quite as important for the military strength of Japan as are questions concerning the training and the equipment of the troops. Military circles observe with grave concern that the country's economic capacity lags behind her military and naval strength. They are therefore actively interested in the destiny of the farmers, the industrial middle classes, the workers—and in the development of export trade. In all these directions they may take a greater part in Japanese politics as soon as their immediate aim—the modernization and increase of the Army and Navy by means of large defence budgets—is in sight. Even then, however, according to Japanese tradition, they may reign indirectly and by proxy; and despite the Army's antagonism towards big business, certain compromises will probably be made with the capitalists, with whom the Army has always co-operated when national issues were at stake.

Military ideas and policies may soon have a decisive influence on Japanese politics.

So far there are no definite economic or political programmes. The Ministry of War, however, published a famous pamphlet in the autumn of 1934. This pamphlet, which was widely distributed and caused the Cabinet great embarrassment, reflects the military point of view, though it does not contain a concrete programme of action. It broadly discusses the future of national defence during the 'international emergency of 1935–6' and beyond, and includes the following statements about Japan's economic position:

> The present economic system has been developed on the basis of individualism. For this reason economic activities tend to serve only individual interests and fancies, and do not always harmonize with the general interests of the State.
>
> The extreme emphasis on free competition may be a danger, arousing antagonism between the classes.
>
> Wealth accumulated by a minority causes misery among the masses, strikes, the failure of small industrial estab-

lishments, the ruin of agriculture; and all these factors upset the balance of our national life.

State control is now barely felt and for this reason it is impossible to mobilize all the forces which would fully exploit our resources, develop our industries, stimulate our foreign trade and direct our economic activities towards a common aim. At the same time the Government Budget is limited, and measures urgently needed in connection with national defence cannot be carried out easily.

Various opinions are current concerning the policies necessary in order to improve economic conditions. From the point of view of national defence the following aims must be kept in mind:

The new economic system must be inspired by the idea of justice for all. It must ensure to everyone a financial return commensurate with his labour, for only thus can personal activity be stimulated and the life of the nation stabilized.

Finance and industry should be co-ordinated so that we can derive the full benefit from our natural resources, our industrial development, our foreign trade and from the measures adopted for national defence.

. . . it is desirable that the people should abandon their individualistic economic conceptions; instead they should recognize the importance of a collective economy; they should work towards the creation of an economic system which will rapidly realize the Empire's ideal.

The State should rigidly control the entire national economy.

Though the importance of industry is not overlooked, the fighting Services are chiefly concerned about agriculture, which is considered the present and future basis of national defence. They are passionately opposed to the theory propagated by many capitalists who believe that

Japanese agriculture is beyond help, and not worth more than palliative measures. Japan's one aim, so these capitalists believe, should be to develop her large industries and, like Great Britain, gradually to abandon her agriculture and her small industries without showing any consideration to either.

In so far as the opponents of this theory, who allege that it is guiding present Government practice, have worked out an alternative, it seems to be as follows: Agriculture must be saved; the industrialization of the country, which must continue, should be based largely on small industries; and an increasing number of such industries should be established in the villages. The surplus agricultural labour would thus be supplied with work, farmers would have an opportunity of supplementing their incomes, and some compensation would be found for the decline in seri-culture. In this way the uprooting of the growing industrial population, with all its social and political consequences, as well as the estrangement between the towns and the villages, might be prevented. With relatively small capital considerable progress could thus be made with further industrialization.

According to military opinion such an 'internal industrial colonization', as it might be called, would be possible only if the entire system of industry, credit, and trade, were co-ordinated and controlled by the State.

Only thus, it is said, can the weakness of small

industries be overcome, only thus can their disadvantages in relation to the larger and more powerful industrial organizations be effectively removed. Only thus can small producers benefit from the growing domestic purchasing power; only thus can the general standard of living be raised. Only thus, in the Army's opinion, can Japan remain Japan, instead of following the example of Western countries and being torn by class war.

The large concerns—and these concerns are very powerful—would oppose the idealists in the Army and Navy if they tried to realize their aims. They claim that their policies are justified by the history of other countries, where economic development has led to growing trustification, to increasingly large industrial organizations and growing urbanization. Can the Japanese Army restrain a similar development in Japan? Would and could the military reformers, whose strength within their own camp is still unknown, go far enough to overcome the resistance of the powerful industrial concerns? No one can as yet answer this question.

The military ideas of a planned economy, however, of an 'internal industrial colonization', would not perhaps be more dangerous to Japan or to the world at large than the present system of a limited '*laisser faire*'.

Japan's population and employment problems are becoming more serious from year to year because of the decay of her agriculture, the growth of her large cities, the concentration and rationalization of her large industries and the resulting danger to her small industries. According to the *Japan Times*, at the third Annual Conference in October 1934 of the Japanese Trade Union Congress a resolution was passed:

> urging the Government to take legislative measures for the protection of workers, referring to the intensification of the impoverishment and distressed conditions in rural districts, which, the resolution claims, were a menace to the standard of living of industrial people, increasing unemployment in urban districts.

These are explosive materials which have already driven forward like rockets Japan's industrial production, export trade and foreign policies, but which might easily lead to more destructive explosions.

The economic development apparently desired by the military reformers, on the other hand, would relieve the pressure of over-population. They would try to raise the standard of living, and work towards greater self-sufficiency. Japan might become stronger within herself without becoming more dangerous to other countries. An increase in exports would still be necessary, but this expansion would be more controlled and less desperate; her domestic competition would be less severe, and working conditions would improve; profits would be more fairly distributed among all classes of producers. Her foreign competitors, too, would be in a better position, for British and other exporters do not suffer as much from the growing volume of Japan's exports as they do from the revolutionary effects of her prices, which are unnecessarily low.

THE ARMY AND WORLD COMPETITION

The propaganda pamphlet of the Japanese Ministry of War contains the following interesting statement about Japanese competition in world markets.

> . . . countries suffering economic stagnation and anxiety concerning the international situation are jealous of the Empire's foreign trade expansion and her growing political power. For this reason these countries have introduced all sorts of measures to curtail Japan's economic and political progress. If nothing is done to counteract these measures, Japanese goods will be driven from foreign markets and Japanese emigrants will find closed doors everywhere; politically, the Empire will be hopelessly isolated, and it is possible that it will be forced to submit to a destiny similar to that of Germany.
>
> From the point of view of the masses, which represent the majority of consumers in the entire world, it is desirable that products should be available on the most favourable conditions possible. From this point of view a country as recently industrialized as Japan enjoys the great advantage of a lower standard of living, whereas countries such as England or the Netherlands are in an unfavourable position. The English and the Dutch favour the small controlling minority in industry and sell their goods at a high price to the coloured population of the colonies. This procedure is contrary to the interests of the masses and to a spirit of fairness. Economic conditions in our Empire, on the other hand, correspond perfectly with the interests of the masses all over the world, so that we must logically become predominant in econo-

mic competition. If English and Dutch competitors should persist in their methods of unlawful competition, the Empire will eventually be obliged to use armed force so that a spirit of fairness may triumph.

We must consider that the commercial drive of England and other countries will be intensified in future. It is easy to predict that the Powers will fling themselves on to the Chinese market in order to offset the difficulties into which the Western world has been plunged. We must therefore reorganize and control the policies governing our foreign trade in the shape of national concentration; private interests must no longer be considered, and, at the same time, we must decide on counter-policies which will enable us to meet the crisis by finding new markets and recovering our old market in China.

JAPAN AND THE WORLD

To-day Japan's export competition is a serious world problem—but the harm which Japan has unwillingly done is often exaggerated, just as the fundamental drawbacks of the post-war economic system are often under-estimated.

With the increase of her exports, Japan drove the 'old' industrial countries from various markets. Japan has done so even in the poorest classes of consumers in the poorest markets, where other countries could never hope to compete with cheap Japanese goods. For unless Japan had invaded these markets, the poor consumers would probably have bought smaller quantities of similar products made in Great Britain or other countries. The masses, whose varied demand is never really satisfied, might also have purchased other industrial goods produced in England or other countries; instead of buying the new Japanese bicycles, for instance, or rubber shoes, they might have purchased hardware or other manufactures of established exporters. At least the masses would have spent their slight surplus with domestic manufacturers who would then have bought more Western goods. Japan's cheap goods did not create a new purchasing power in these markets; she merely absorbed existing purchasing power, which would otherwise have benefited her competitors.

It is true, however, that the world as a whole has won at least as much as she has lost by Japan's progress. For Japan always buys a little more from foreign countries than she sells to them. Workers in Great Britain and in many other countries have virtually lost their jobs to Japanese workers, but increasing Japanese imports of raw materials have supplied work for Australian wool growers, for Indian and American cotton farmers, for rubber planters, for lumbermen, and for miners in many other countries. As a result, many of these countries, in turn, supplied the industrial workers of Great Britain and other countries with larger orders and more work than would have been available without Japanese imports. Here Japan has created a new purchasing power; from this point of view she has not intensified but alleviated the world depression.

In money values Japan has contributed at least

as much to world trade as she has got from it. Japan, as a country, has not been enriched by her increasing exports; she has not accumulated reserves, and she has not acquired one ounce of gold as a national profit. As far as material value and labour are concerned, she has probably given far more than she has received. She exports at extraordinarily low prices, whereas she imports at relatively high prices. She maintains her balance of trade by making national sacrifices, which cannot be estimated in figures, but which must be very great. These financial sacrifices do not come from an abundance of wealth, but from desperate need.

Japan is fully justified in not considering herself a debtor, and much less a delinquent in the world economic system.

The countries which Japan provided with work, and those from which she took it are, however, not identical. Roughly speaking, it is the manufacturing countries who have been harmed by Japan, while the raw-materials countries have been benefited. Japan has therefore upset the balance of the world economic system, a balance which was not too stable in any case. This is the real reason why other countries complain about her; and the fear of her increasing exports is really an anxiety that she will upset this balance still more.

The organization of world trade has shown itself to be too rigid to cope with disturbances of this kind. That fact is, in Japan's view, responsible for the difficulties now confronting industrial countries.

Theoretically, at least, it is easy to imagine a remedy for Japan's disturbing effect on the world: the expansion of world trade should be organized on a co-operative plan, so that old-timers and new-comers can develop, so that prosperity will be restored in the West and in the East.

The world is, however, growing more and more nationalistic; it is suspicious, and more than ever dominated by antagonisms and misunderstandings. At present the only hope lies in a natural recovery of international trade, a recovery which will surmount man-made obstacles. . . .

In the meantime the bitter struggle for markets continues.

Printed in Great Britain by Butler & Tanner Ltd., Frome and London